# the Little"O"

Or may we cram
Within this wooden *O* the very casques
That did affright the air at Agincourt?
For 'tis your thoughts that now
        must deck our kings,
Jumping o'er times,
Turning the accomplishments of many years
Into an hour-glass   *—(Shakespeare)*

# the Little "O"

Merlin J. Guilfoyle, D.D., J.C. D.
Bishop of Stockton

Publishers

willow house

Stockton, California

Library of Congress Catalog Card No. 72-86757
ISBN: 9-912-450-05-3
Printed in the United States of America

## PROCEDAMUS IN PACE

Be Thou my *walking shoes*, O Lord
When pilgrims go out tramping
Throughout the world of Europe.
I'd like to walk to Greece and Rome
    Some day before I die.
Be Thou my *burro or camel*, O Lord
From Galilee to Egypt,
From sea to Jordan River.
I'd love to ride the Holy Land
    Some day before I die.
Be Thou my rolling *train*, O Lord,
Alas trains now are fading,
Across Mongolia, Russia, too.
I'd like to see all Orient
    Some day before I die.
Be Thou my sailing *ship*, O Lord
Upon the foaming oceans,
From zone to zone a rolling.
I'd love to sail the Antipodes
    Some day before I die.
Be Thou my *aeroplane*, O Lord
The narrow oceans flying,
From pole to pole awinging.
I'd love to touch Antartica
    Some day before I die.
Be Thou *machine with gas*, O Lord
To visit homes and mountains,
The deserts, shores and valleys.
I'd love to see America
    Some day before I die.

# Contents

# Forward

After volumes concerning San Francisco, California, and the United States, it seemed proper to project a fourth book looking at other parts of our globe.

Volume One, "San Francisco, No Mean City," is a title suggested by another Bishop, Paul, who said: "I am a citizen of no mean city." The author therefore reflects on the seagulls, earthquakes, the fog, pigeons, Archbishop Alemany, and cable cars.

The city of St. Francis means Mission Dolores, the cemetery and Basilica, Portsmouth Square, the bridges, James Flood, Jasper O'Farrell who laid out the streets, and Monsignor Ramm, who lived at the Cathedral for 54 years.

There are likewise chapters which speak of the ferry boats, and the donkeys of Golden Gate Park. We think of George Fennel, the poet of the Palace Hotel, the Little Sisters of the Poor, the 77 hills and Van Ness Avenue.

Life by the Golden Gate includes the City Hall, the Street Monuments, Las Pulgas (i.e., fleas), the Tivoli Theater, the YMI, fog horns, Angel Island, and Alcatraz. Yes, St. Francis and St. Paul look down upon no mean city.

The *second volume,* "California, State of Grace," continues the sentence of Paul, the Bishop: "I am a citizen of Tarsus, in Salicia." It is San Francisco, California.

California is called the State of Grace, as explained in chapters on the 21 Missions, the National and State paradisal parks. The Golden State is oranges, grapes and artichokes as described by a native son. Reflections are made on the quail, the poppy, plums and rainbow trout.

The State is Father Serra's rosary and Marysland. Lines on California architecture and adobe continue our story under six flags. California means the Seals, who became the Giants; her relief map includes Yosemite, volcanic Lassen and the Farallones.

The description continues with swallows, dams and trams, the redwoods, and the California volunteers. Indeed, it is a State of Grace, from Los Angeles to San Francisco, to Blessed Sacramento.

The *third book* is "Of Thee I Sing, The American Cathedral." This edifice contains Niagara Falls, the Statue of Liberty, and the Liberty Bell. America means baseball and the Gettysburg Address, the Washington Monument, and the buffalo nickel.

America grew through several stages as told in chapters on the Indian, the Confederate poet, voting, and the convention of the Donkey and the Elephant. The United States includes Carlsbad Caverns and Mammoth Cave, automobiles and the first A-bomb.

The United States means chapters on the little red schoolhouse and the woodshed, the possibility of having 50 wives, the addition of Alaska and Hawaii. It seems good to conclude this book with a column on Thanksgiving Day.

A San Franciscan, native son of the Golden West, Yankee, is also catholic, universal. He is interested in all men of the human family. Therefore, *this fourth volume* speaks of this burnt out star, this "Little O."

Australia has the koala bear and France the Cathedral of Chartres. There are the cedars of Lebanon and the Colosscum in Italy, which surrounds Vatican State. There is a Santa Claus in Russia and a Mecca to Fatima. Germany has the Dom of Cologne, and England a channel which the French call La Manche.

Poland is dedicated to the Black Virgin of Czestachowa, and the cedars of Lebanon are not far from the Holy Land. Although we speak Greek in our English, we also have ties with Africa, China, and the Wild Geese of Ireland.

The well worn expression, "It's a small world," holds in one embrace the Stone of Scone, Fuji of the Rising Sun and Malta of St. Paul's shipwreck. Our Lady of Guadalupe is Empress of all the Americas.

A gypsy may be from Egypt, but there is also a road to the Philippines. Switzerland has the St. Bernard dog and Damascus, Syria, the street called Straight. St. Lawrence is a river of Canada, and the Ganges flows through India.

St. Stephen looks on Budapest and martyred Hungary. San Martin is the hero of South America, the Escorial is the pride of Spain. These and other countries the author will visit with you from the South Seas to the Seven Wonders of the World.

Slav, Teuton, Kelt, I count them all
       My friends and brother souls,
With all the peoples, great and small,
       That dwell between the poles.
              — Alfred Lord Tennyson

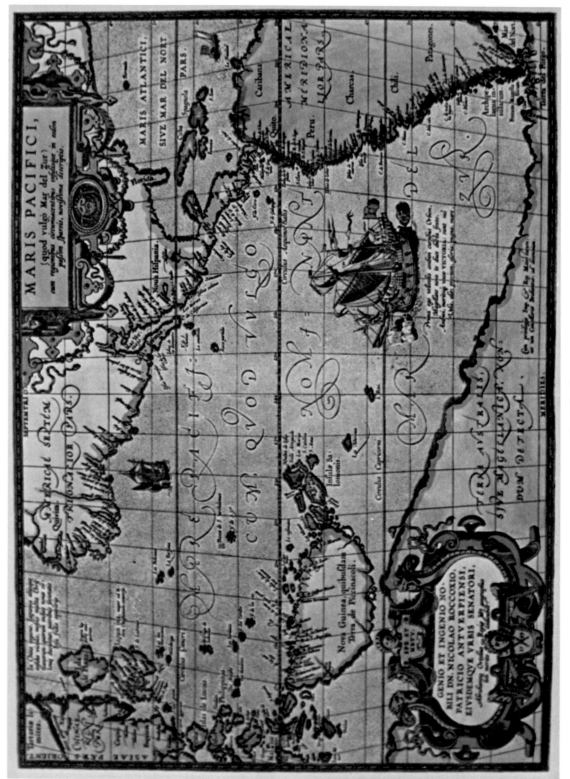

*My Pilgrimage*

# Itinerarium

The man of the world starts out on a journey with traveler's insurance. Our more practical Mother, the Church, advocates what is known as the Itinerarium. This is a collection of prayers for the traveler, which is printed in a priest's breviary.

In the earliest days of the Church, the Fathers of the Desert, St. Anthony and St. Pachomius, established regulations for monks on a journey. The Rule of St. Basil contains prescriptions for monastic travel.

St. Benedict commanded the brethren who were about to make a journey, to first commend themselves to the prayers of the abbot and the community. If it were to be a short trip, they simply asked for the abbot's blessing and the prayers of the community. A longer journey was begun with special hymns, blessings and the kiss of peace, while the travelers knelt on the steps of the altar.

## Our Absent Brethren

To this day the Litany of the Saints contains the petition, "Let us pray for our absent brethren." The prayers of the Divine Office conclude, "May the divine help remain always with us."

The Ceremonial Book of Bishops prescribes that the prelate should recite, with his chaplains and household, the Itinerary Prayers. The rubric, or rule in red ink, which introduces the hymn, states: "The bishop about to undertake a journey, begins the following antiphon before he climbs on his horse."

The priest, setting out on a journey, reads from his Breviary: "May the Lord, the almighty and merciful, lead us into the way of peace and prosperity, and may the angel Raphael be with us on our way, that we may return home again in peace, and health and gladness."

The biblical book of Tobias tells of the solicitude of the angel Raphael during the journey of the young man.

The prayer continues with a reference to the journey of the Children of Israel across the Red Sea on the way to the Promised Land.

There is recollection of the Christmas Star, which guided the three wise men to the crib at Bethlehem.

> Then the Kings rode out of the city gate,
> With a clatter of hoofs in proud array;
> But they went not back to Herod the Great,
> For they knew his malice and feared his hate,
> And returned to their homes by another way.
> — Henry Longfellow

1

The world may say, "Bon Voyage," "Au Revoir," "Aloha," "Good Luck," "Pleasant Journey." But it is difficult to find more fitting words at the moment of departure than those of our Mother the Church.

> Be unto us, O Lord, a help when we go forward, a
> comfort by the way, a shadow from the heat, a covering
> from the rain and the cold, a chariot in weariness, a
> refuge in trouble, a staff in slippery paths, a harbor
> in shipwreck.
> Do Thou lead us, that we may happily reach
> our destination, and thereafter come again safe unto our
> own home.

Whoever has had the opportunity to drive Sisters in an automobile has often realized that the nuns too have an Itinerarium. It differs with various communities, but it follows the same pattern.

## Back Seat Driver

You step on the starter, only to hear from the back seat a sorority supplication, "Lord have mercy on us, Christ have mercy on us." As you release the brake, your back seat drivers declare, "From a sudden and unprovided death, deliver us O Lord." When you are about "to bless" the lady driver in front of you, you are prevented by the supplication, "Let us proceed in peace. In the name of the Lord."

> As life runs on, the road grows strange
> With faces new, and near the end
> The milestones into headstones change,
> 'Neath every one a friend.
> — James Lowell

Even on Good Friday, Our Mother the Church prays for travelers, just before she unveils the cross. "Let us pray, most dearly beloved, to God the Father Almighty, to give to travelers safe return, to the sick restoration to health, and to those who are at sea secure harbourage."

The nostalgia of the traveler reminds us that we shall always be homesick until we reach heaven.

> If there's a heaven upon the earth, a
> fellow knows it when
> He's been away from home a week, and
> then gets back again.
> — Will Carleton

2

## Going Home

The Church never prays for physical comforts except in so far as they lead to heaven. So she concludes her supplications for travelers with: "Order the goings of Thy servants in the safe path that leads unto salvation in Thee, that amidst all the manifold changes of this life's pilgrimage, Thy shield may always be with us."

Give me my scallop-shell of quiet,
My staff of faith to walk upon,
My scrip of joy, immortal diet,
My bottle of salvation,
My gown of glory, hope's true gage,
And thus I'll take my pilgrimage.

Blood must be my body's balmer;
        No other balm will there be given:
Whilst my soul, like quiet palmer,
        Travelleth towards the land of heaven.
                    — Sir Walter Raleigh

Magic Numbers

# Seven Wonders

All of the seven wonders of the world enumerated on the list of Philo, the Greek philosopher, were man-made. All likewise have disappeared with the exception of the pyramids.

> The Pyramids first, which in Egypt were laid;
> Next Babylon's Garden, for Amytis made;
> Then Mausolos' Tomb of affection and guilt;
> Fourth, the Temple of Dian in Ephesus built;
> Then Colossus of Rhodes, cast in brass, to the sun;
> Sixth, Jupiter's statue, by Phydias done;
> The Pharos of Egypt comes last, we are told,
> Or the Palace of Cyrus, cemented with gold.

About 5000 years ago, the great pyramid of Cheops was constructed of limestone, with smooth white sides. It was 480 feet in height and the length of each base was 755 ft. There are about 70 pyramids in Egypt, but this wonder of the world covers 13 acres. The nearby Sphinx, half-man and half-lion, is perhaps the oldest object constructed by man. It is 140 ft. long, with a head 30 ft. from crown to chin.

## Pyramids and Sphinx

The Grecian Sphinx used to devour all citizens, who could not solve this riddle:

What goes on four feet, on two feet, and three,
But the more feet it goes on the weaker it be?

The quiz was answered by Oedipus with the reply, "Man." For an infant crawls on all fours, in manhood goes erect on his two feet, and in old age supports his tottering legs with a cane.

The second wonder of the world was a statue of Zeus. It was made of hammered gold with flesh parts of ivory by Phidias, the greatest of Grecian artists. This 60 ft. statue was taken to Constantinople where it was destroyed by the great fire in 475.

The third wonder was the Colossus of the island of Rhodes. This gigantic statue was 105 ft. high, a war memorial of the defense of Rhodes which was constructed from the warlike engines abandoned by the enemy. It gives us the word colossal and colosseum.

Exaggerated stories told of ships that sailed between its legs astride the harbor. Therefore Cassius says of Julius Caesar:

Why, man, he doth bestride the narrow world
Like a Colossus, and we petty men
Walk under his huge legs and peep about
To find ourselves dishonourable graves.

## Mausoleum

The fourth world wonder was a tomb erected in 353 B.C. by a queen of Asia Minor. Marble columns sustained a pyramid which was topped by a marble chariot. This sepulchral monument in honor of King Mausolus gives us the name mausoleum.

Four times as high as the Colossus was the Pharos lighthouse at Alexandria, another world wonder.

The temple of Diana at Ephesus, made of white marble, was also one of the seven wonders. St. Paul preached at this pagan shrine in a city where soon a General Council would salute Mary as the Mother of God.

Babylon, where Daniel was liberated from the lions' den and where Belshazzar asked for an interpretation of the handwriting on the wall, produced the seventh wonder. It is said that there Nebuchadnezzar built the Hanging Gardens to gratify his wife, who was weary of the flat plains and homesick for hills.

In 550 A.D. St. Gregory enumerated Seven Wonders of God's creation, rather than the perishable seven things made by man. He marveled at the tides, seeds, springs, a volcano, the cycle of the sun, the orbit of the moon, and the phoenix bird.

6

## Seven Supernaturals

However, the seven wonders of the world are neither the work of the ancient, nor the natural creations of God. The seven astounding wonders of life are known as sacraments — seven visible signs which produce inward grace. All the strategic moments of life are served by Baptism, Penance, Confirmation, Holy Eucharist, the Anointing of the Sick, Holy Orders and Matrimony.

The Wonder of all time is Jesus Christ, born of the Virgin Mary, true God and true Man. Seven times the Church salutes Him in her night prayers from Dec. 17 to Dec. 23. O Wisdom! O Leader! O Adonai! O Root of Jesse! O Orient! O King of Nations! O Key of David! O Emmanuel, God with Us!

The first joy of Mary was the joy of one:
That the blessed Jesus was born to be her Son.
The next joy of Mary was the joy of two:
That her Son Jesus could read the Scripture through.
The next joy of Mary was the joy of three:
That her Son Jesus could make the blind to see.
The next joy of Mary was the joy of four:
That her Son Jesus could turn the rich to poor.
The next joy of Mary was the joy of five:
That her Son Jesus could raise the dead alive.
The next joy of Mary was the joy of six:
That her Son Jesus could bear the crucifix.
The last joy of Mary was the joy of seven:
That her Son Jesus could open the gates of heaven.

*Sceptered Isle*

# The English Sleeve

This English channel is 22 miles wide from Dover to Calais. France has a much more extensive shore than England on this body of water. To the French, therefore, it is not the English channel, but La Manche, "The Sleeve."

The first man to swim from Dover to Calais was Captain Matthew Webb, who made the crossing in 1875. His efforts consumed 21 hours and 45 minutes.

Gertrude Ederle was the first woman to swim the channel. She set a record of 14 hours and 34 minutes on August 6, 1926, a time since lowered by several men.

## The Channel Challenge

Various motives have prompted men to swim across the natural barrier of water. Story has it that Leander navigated the Hellespont each night to keep a date with Hero. There is no record of his time.

> It was a tall young oysterman
>     lived by the river-side.
> His shop was just upon the bank,
>     his boat was on the tide.
> The daughter of a fisherman,
>     that was so straight and slim,
> Lived over on the other bank,

right opposite to him.
"I read it in the story book,
    that for to kiss his dear,
Leander swam the Hellespont —
    and I will swim this here."
             — Oliver W. Holmes

Many years ago the Romans crossed over from the continent to the British Isles. On the white cliffs of Dover there is a lighthouse of Roman masonry. There is a cruciform church with arches of Roman bricks.

The sea is calm tonight,
The tide is full, the moon lies fair
Upon the straits. On the French
    coast the light
Gleams and is gone; the cliffs of
    England stand
Glimmering and vast, out in the
    tranquil bay.
             — Matthew Arnold

It was Pope Gregory the Great who planned to invade Anglo-Saxon England, then sunk in idolatry. He picked 30 monks from the monastery of St. Andrew on the Coelian Hill. With their prior, St. Augustine, they set out from Rome in 596 with letters of introduction to the Bishops of French cities.

## The Sceptered Isle

These missionaries crossed the Sleeve and landed on the Isle of Thanet, governed by Ethelbert, King of Kent. This king was a pagan, but his wife, Bertha, was a devout French Christian. The monks were given a dwelling at Canterbury and in 597 the king himself was baptized.

For centuries the inhabitants of this isle sat secure from the destruction of major military campaigns.

This royal throne of kings, this sceptered isle,
This other Eden, demi-paradise,
This fortress built by Nature for herself
Against infection and the hand of war,
This happy breed of men, this little world,
This precious stone set in the silver sea,
Which serves it in the office of a wall

10

Or as a moat defensive to a house,
Against the envy of less happier lands
This blessed plot, this earth, this realm, this England.
                                        — Richard II



   Yet there were many sea battles on this sleeve of water. In the important battle of Dover, fought on August 21, 1217, the English threw unslaked lime into the face of the French and confounded them with arrows.
   As early as 1802 Napoleon dreamed of a tunnel to England. In 1880 an underwater link was actually begun. On the chalk cliffs of Folkestone there is a shaft 2000 yards long, about 5 feet high. It was the aborted dream of statesmen and engineers.

## White Cliffs

   The crossing, now envisioned by engineers, would compose two railway tunnels. Below 180 feet of water is a chalk bed through which the bore would be made at 270 feet below the surface. Approaches from Cap Gris Nez and Folkestone would make the tunnel about 30 miles long.
   The military position of England is no longer important as an island fortress. The airplane and guided missiles have dried up the Sleeve. Nuclear weapons have shrunk the globe so that even the oceans appear as channels. Only world peace insures any local tranquillity.
   The waters of the sea still wash the cliffs; the line of empire, built on floating forts, has been breached by time. Was Shakespeare a prophet? He lived at Stratford-on-Avon.

This land of such dear souls,
        this dear dear land,
Dear for her reputation
        through the world,
Is now leased out, I die
        pronouncing it,
Like a tenement or pelting farm.
England, bound in with the
        triumphant sea,
Whose rocky shore beats back the
        envious siege
Of watery Neptune, is now bound
        in with shame,
With inky blots and rotten
        parchment bonds.

That England that was wont to
conquer others,
Hath made a shameful conquest
of itself.

England will ever live in such names as Magna Charta and Piccadilly, the Canterbury Tales and the Old Lady of Threadneedle Street. What history is told in Plymouth Hoe of the Mayflower and Francis Drake, in Old Bailey, Westminster Abbey, Windsor Castle, Big Ben and Buckingham Palace. Nelson looks down on Trafalgar Square and back to the trilithons of Stonehenge. The sceptered isle has seen the Thames, London Bridge, the Beefeaters of the Tower, St. Paul's Cathedral, the White Horse, the round table of King Arthur and cricket.

Englishmen all were St. Thomas a Becket, St. Thomas More, St. John Fisher, and John Henry Cardinal Newman.

"The Giftie gie us."

# Stone of Scone

Among the many crimes referred to Scotland Yard was the theft of the Stone of Scone, supposedly stolen by the Scotch. The name Scotland Yard has become a trademark, like Sherlock Holmes or the FBI. There is a short street in London, off Whitehall, which was the headquarters of the metropolitan police from 1829-1890. On this street was the palace where the Scottish kings used to lodge when recreating in England; it was the yard of the Scots.

The stone which became the concern of the Yard was stolen, or liberated, from Westminster Abbey. The history runneth thus.

Edward I hoped for a union of England and Scotland and for this purpose he negotiated a marriage between Margaret of the Scots and his son. However, the eight-year-old queen died while visiting Norway, and two gentlemen claimed the throne.

Edward became the umpire of the dispute; he favored a certain Baliol, hoping to receive some help in his war with France. But the Scotch, au contraire as the French say, allied with France.

## Coronation Chair

Edward thereupon invaded Scotland, deposed Baliol, and returned with the coronation Stone of Scone. This stone rested in the old Abbey in Perthshire, where the ancient Scottish kings were crowned.

If Fates go right, where'er this stone is found,
The Scots shall monarchs of that realm be crowned.

From that time the stone was in Westminster Abbey, where it participated in the coronation ceremony of English kings. However it belongs to Scots like Sir Walter Scott, Robert Bruce, Sir James Barrie, Robert Burns, Robert Louis Stevenson, James Watt, Alexander Graham Bell, and Andrew Carnegie. It stirs up images of Mary Queen of Scots, Holy Rood, kilted highlanders, tossing the caber, and Loch Lomond.

Scotland is Edinburgh Castle, the Firth of Forth, Scotch collies and whisky, the thistle, tweeds and tartans; it is Melrose Abbey and Auld Brig o' Doon, bagpipes and lakes of the Trossachs.

The sleuths of Scotland Yard followed clues, obvious to Doctor Watson, stooge of Sherlock Holmes. The stolen object is 2 feet long, nearly 3 feet wide and 1 foot thick. The purloined pebble is by weight about 21 stone — some 300 pounds.

The trophy had been securely clamped with strong irons underneath the coronation chair. The rogues who lifted the relic, broke a splinter off the coronation throne in the robbery. The detectives further noted that the thieves had entered by the Poet's Corner and made their escape by dragging the Stone of Scone over the graves of poets, of Tennyson who wrote:

Ah! when shall all mens' good
Be each man's rule, and universal peace
Lie like a shaft of light across the land
And like a lane of beams athwart the sea,
Through all the circle of the golden year.

The theft of the Coronation Stone had been the most sensational robbery since Colonel Blood almost carried off the crown jewels from the Tower of London. There are those who rate the theft of the crown from Edward VIII, by the twice divorced Wallis Warfield Simpson, as the greatest shock to English face, (to use a Japanese expression), since Henry VIII's matrimonial hopalong ventures.

## Tara and Jacob

This is the history of this Stone of Destiny. Story tells us that the stone is neither English, nor Scotch, but Irish. The ancient name for Eire was Innisfail, which means Stone of Destiny. It is said that this was brought to Ireland from Arabia and was used at Tara for the coronation of Irish kings.

16

No more to chiefs and ladies bright
The harp of Tara swells:
The chord alone, that breaks at night,
Its tale of ruin tells.

Thus Freedom now so seldom wakes,
The only throb she gives
Is when some heart indignant breaks,
To show that still she lives.   ·
— Thomas Moore

It further develops that the stone is not Irish but Jewish. It is supposed to be the very pillow on which Jacob rested. In the words of Holy Scripture: "He took of the stones that lay there, and putting them under his head, slept in the same place. And he saw in his sleep a ladder standing upon the earth, and the top thereof touching heaven, the Angels of God ascending and descending by it."

An English poet, broken by vice and poverty, once thought of this stone, and wrote:

The angels keep their ancient places: —
Touch but a stone, and start a wing!
'Tis ye, 'tis your estranged faces,
That miss the many-splendoured thing.
But (when so sad thou cans't not sadder)
Cry; and upon thy so sore loss
Shall shine the traffic of Jacob's ladder
Pitched between Heaven and Charing Cross.

## Altar Stone

But Francis Thompson had an assumption from his weakness. He wrote beautifully of Mary, calling her "Jacob's Ladder."

Her soul from earth to Heaven lies,
Like the ladder of the vision,
      Whereon go
      To and fro,
In ascension and demission,
Star-flecked feet of Paradise.

This Stone of Scone has been recovered by Scotland Yard but it will eventually disappear from history. The only Stone of Destiny is the altar stone, the tomb of martyrs, on which the Holy Sacrifice has been offered.

*Na Geana Fiadhaine*

# Exiles of Eire

The Hierarchy of Ireland once set aside the first Sunday in October as a day of special prayer for Irish emigrants. This action of the Bishops reminded us that Ireland is much greater than the island. The motherland of Eire calls her exiles Na Geana Fiadhaine, "The Wild Geese."

The name of the Gael is found in every country. There were Don Ricardo Wall, prime minister of Spain, Count Peter Lucy of Russia, Field Marshal Brown of Austria, County Lally of India. Among many in European diplomacy we may recall Tyrconnell, O'Mahony, Lawless, and De Lacy.

## Wild Geese

In the New World the generalissimo of the armies which prepared the way of Padre Serra in California was Count Alejandro O'Reilly. The overland trail, the Tahoe and Carson pass, were opened by Thomas Fitzpatrick. Lest the litany be longer than that of all the saints, there was finally Tim Murphy of Wexford, who became Don Timoteo, Alcalde of San Rafael.

> War-battered dogs are we,
> Fighters in every clime;
> Fillers of trench and grave,
> Mockers bemocked by time.
> War-dogs hungry and grey,

Gnawing a naked bone,
Fighters in every clime —
Every cause by our own.
                    — Emily Lawless


There is an interesting history about nine wild geese, whose goose was almost cooked. The solemn voice of the presiding judge called off in rote:

"John Mitchell, Morris Lyene, Patrick Donahue, Thomas McGee, Charles Duffy, Thomas Meagher, Richard O'Gorman, Terrence McManus, Michael Ireland — have you anything to say before the court passes sentence?"

With a touch of blarney Thomas Meagher spoke: "My lord, this is our first offense, but not our last. If you will be easy with us this once, we promise on our word as gentlemen to try to do better the next time. And the next time, sure we won't be fools enough to be caught."

## Far From the Land

Public protest from all parts of the world produced a commutation of the death penalty from Queen Victoria. Life imprisonment in the penal colonies of Australia was the substitute. The wild geese had been put to flight.

Thou shalt leave each thing
Beloved most dearly; this is the first shaft
Shot from the bow of exile. Thou shalt prove
How salt the taste is of other's bread
How hard the passage to descend and climb
By other's stairs.
                    — Dante

Man proposes, but God disposes; history works out the divine plan. In 1874, Australia elected a Prime Minister; his name was Charles Duffy, one of the nine wild geese. Whither had the other eight flown?

The history of the flock reads in this wise: Meagher, governor of Montana; O'Gorman, governor general of Newfoundland, and Morris Lyene, his successor; McManus, brigadier general of the U.S. Army; Mitchell, New York politician; Donahue, American brigadier; McGee, council-president of the Dominion of Canada.

Roll back the portals of silence. Summon her
        dead men forth
From Munster and Connacht and Leinster and the
        proud, dark hills of the north!
Blare to the breezes of morning, a reveille,

wild and free,
To waken her slumbering Wild Geese
wherever their ashes be.

Where do wild geese come from and whither do they go? In the plan of the Creator, birds give glory by following instinctive flight. Sure He Who said, "Consider the birds of the air . . . how much more valuable are you than they," has a plan for His Wild Geese.

He who from zone to zone
Guides through the distant sky my certain flight
In the long way which I must tread alone,
Will guide my steps aright.
— William Bryant

## Missionaries All

It has been the mission of the Exiles of Eire to carry the message of the Faith with their migrations. On the Feast of the Holy Rosary, which is recited by the family in Irish homes each night, the Bishops once requested this additional prayer:

"O Jesus, Who, in the first days of Thy life on earth, was compelled to leave the land of Thy birth, and with Mary, Thy loving Mother, and St. Joseph, to endure in Egypt the hardships and poverty of emigrants, turn Thine eyes in mercy upon our people who, in search of employment, are forced to leave their native land.

Far away from all that is dear to them, and faced with the difficulties of a new life, they are often exposed to grave temptation and dangers to the salvation of their souls.

Be Thou, O Lord, their guide upon their way, their support, their strength in temptation. Keep them loyal to their Faith, free from sin and faithful to all their family ties."

The Wild Geese shall return and we'll welcome
them home.
So active, so armed, so flighty,
A flock was ne'er known to this island to come
Since the days of Prince Fionn the mighty.

They shall return to the lakes of Killarney and the Giants' Causeway, to the peat bog, the turf fire and the Blarney stone. They will come back to Erin — to Parknasilla with its subtropical plants, to the potatoes, and the shamrocks, to where the River Shannon flows and the sun rises over Galway Bay. They return to hurling, to horses and to Gaelic football. The flock returns to the Book of Kells, to the isle of saints and scholars — to Patrick, Bridget, and Columkill.

Notre Dame

# Mary's Windows

Throughout the world there can be found much beauty in many parts; in the cathedral of Chartres, France, there is a beautiful whole. The Cathedral of Chartres is not the product of architects only, or glass workers, or sculptors; it is the work of souls, who knew the Virgin. A letter written in 1145, tells us the secret; the stones were carried from the quarries five miles away:

"Who has ever heard tell, that powerful princes, nobles, men and women, have bent their proud and haughty necks to the harness of carts, they have dragged to the abode of Christ all that is necessary for the construction of the church? When they halt, nothing is heard but the confession of sins, and pure and suppliant prayer to God to obtain pardon. There one sees old people, young people, little children."

## Stones Speak

The Cathedral of Chartres is about 509 feet long, 210 feet wide; the church will accommodate about 15,000 people.

As Chesterton said: "Christ prophesied the whole of Gothic architecture in that hour when nervous and respectable people objected to the shouting of Jerusalem. He said, 'If these were silent the very stones would cry out.' Under the impulse of His spirit arose like a clamorous chorus the facades of the medieval cathedrals, thronged with shouting faces and open mouths. The prophecy has fulfilled itself; the very stones cry out."

The glory of Chartres is glass. The use of glass is perhaps oriental in origin, for the art came to Venice from the East. Glass is said to be stained when it is colored by metallic oxide, or by burning some pigment into the surface. The colored glass is then arranged in designs or mosaics, so that the light, passing through the window forms a picture. This art began some time in the eleventh century, but later degenerated into the cruder style of mere painted windows.

## Tree of Jesse

In the north lancet of Chartres Cathedral is the Tree of Jesse, a window considered the best work of stained glass in the world. The name of the cathedral is Notre Dame, and so this beautiful window wishes to show that Mary, the Mother of God, was of the royal line of David, as foretold by the prophets: "Obed begot Jesse, Jesse begot David the King ... And David begot Joseph, the husband of Mary, and of her was born Jesus, who is called Christ."

The secret of stained glass is said to be the color blue; blue is light, and light is the law of a perfect window. Chartres is Mary's and blue belongs to the Virgin. Why is the Blessed Virgin clad in blue?

> Because when comes no cloud between
> My heart and heaven above
> Then wears the firmament serene
> The livery of love.
> — Father Tabb

Although the nave of this church is almost 53 feet, the rose window of the west front is about 44 feet in diameter. The rose window therefore takes up almost the whole expanse, for this is Mary's home, and the rose is the sign of the Blessed Virgin. Dante prays to Mary "that beauteous flower whom I ever invoke, morning and evening."

> Virgin mother, daughter of thy son,
> lowly and uplifted more than any creature.
> Thou art she, who didst human nature so ennoble,
> that its own Maker scorned not to become its making.
> Thy kindness not only helps one who asks, but oftentimes
> freely foreruns the request.

## Atomic Frustration

One of the greatest poems of the millions made to Mary is the Prayer to the Virgin of Chartres by Henry Adams. He traces the defection

24

of history from Mary and her Son. He interposes a Prayer to the Atom. Frustrated, he and the human race realize the need of a Mother and a Redeemer.

So I too wandered off among the host
That racked the earth to find the Father's clue.
I did not find the Father, but I lost
What now I value more, the Mother, — You!

What are we then? the lords of space?
The master-mind whose tasks you do?
Jockey who rides you in the race?
Or are we atoms whirled apace,
Shaped and controlled by you?

Seize, then, the Atom! rack his joints!
Tear out of him his secret spring!
Grind him to nothing! — though he points
to us, and his life-blood anoints
Me — the dead Atom-King!

A curious prayer, dear Lady! is it not?
Strangely unlike the prayers I prayed to you!
Stranger because you find me at this spot,
Here, at your feet, asking your help anew.

La Belle France suggests Paris, Notre Dame Cathedral and the Montmartre, the Madeleine, Place de l'opera, Cafe de la Paix, the Place de la Concorde, the Seine, the Arch of Triumph and the Louvre, the Eiffel Tower and the Champs Elysees. What pages of history turn over with the names Fontainebleau, Versailles and Napoleon Bonaparte! France is the country of Marseille, Carcassonne and the bridge of Avignon. It means recreation on the Riviera or Mont Blanc, and death on the beaches of Normandy. Good food, cheese, perfume, gloves, porcelain, Bordeaux wine, Champagne and Chartreuse are products of the land.

The eldest daughter of the Church gave birth to King Clovis, Charlemagne, Joan of Arc and Reims, Sacre Coeur and St. Margaret Mary, the Cure of Ars, Mount Saint Michel and Bernadette of Lourdes.

*La pluma es lengua del alma*
*(Don Quixote)*

# El Escorial

It was on April 23, 1563, that the first stone of the colossal Escorial was laid. This famous edifice is situated 35 miles from Madrid, where Philip II began its construction in memory of his father, Charles I. He gave it the name of San Lorenzo, because on the feast of St. Lawrence the Spanish were victorious in the battle of St. Quintin.

The name "escorial" is said to come from the dross of a nearby smithery so that the proper title of this remarkable construction is El Real Monasterio de San Lorenzo del Escorial.

Some have seen in the edifice the form a gridiron, the instrument of martyrdom for St. Lawrence. It is really a combination of many structures, for the Escorial is a basilica, a monastery, a palace, and a pantheon.

The church is of stone with Doric simplicity; an immense dome and tall towers point it out from a distance. The tabernacle is marble of several colors; the choir chairs and retable of the altar are the work of Juan de Herrera. The metal statues of the screen were cast by Pompeo Leoni.

For many years the monastery nearby housed the Hieronymite monks. This congregation was an amalgamation of hermits whom the Popes united under the rule of St. Augustine, while the name St. Jerome was kept as patron. In 1885 the Augustinians were given custody of the Escorial.

## Royal Pantheon

The living kings of Spain also occupied a part of the Escorial. Indeed, Philip II had an opening made in the wall of his room adjoining the chapel in order that he might look at the Holy Sacrifice of the Mass from his sick bed.

The dead kings likewise remain in a kind of royal pantheon under the chapel. With the exception of Philip V and Ferdinand VI, all the kings since Charles I are entombed in this mausoleum. Here, too, lies one of history's most triumphant heroes, the last son of Emperor Charles V, and half brother of King Philip, known in history as Don Juan of Austria.

> Where, risen from a doubtful seat
> and half attainted stall,
> The last knight of Europe takes
> weapons from the wall.
> Don Juan pounding from the
> slaughter-painted poop,
> Purpling all the ocean like a
> bloody pirate's sloop.
> Vivat Hispania!
> Domino Gloria!
> Don Juan of Austria
> Has set his people free.
>                 — G. K. Chesterton

The Escorial shelters not only the remains of kings but the learning of many great minds from the entire civilized world. It houses some 35,000 volumes with 4600 manuscripts. Priceless manuscripts are in Arabic, Greek, and Latin, some with rich illuminations.

## Cultural Museum

This treasure house contains also tapestries by Goya, Bayeux, and Alonso Cano. Paintings of many famous artists abound under such names as Holbein, Tintoretto, Titian, Giordano, Goya, Reni, and Ribera. Murals and musical compositions add to this shangri-la of learning.

The building of the Escorial took more than 21 years. It is one of the wonders of the world with 120 miles of corridor, 16 courtyards, 88 fountains, 15 cloisters, 1200 doors, 2673 windows, 3000 cells, 86 staircases, and 3000 feet of painted fresco.

We of California do not have to be reminded that countless lands are designated by Spanish names. San Fernando, for example, is a common name on the coast, but not all Native Sons recognize him as King of Castile and Leon. Relieving the march between San Gabriel and San

Buenaventura was Mission San Fernando Rey de Espada, founded on September 8, 1797.

Saint Ferdinand spent much of his life in liberating Christians from the unbelievers of Islam. Yet he could honestly say: "Thou, O Lord, Who searchest the heart of man, Thou knowest that I desire Thy glory, not mine, and the increase of Thy faith and holy religion, not of any temporal kingdom." He entered battle with a large picture of the Blessed Virgin carried before him and a small one attached to his saddle.

> Thy knights, O Queen, ride forth
>     by east and west
> By south and north through all
>     the world they ride;
> By town and hamlet, coast and countryside
> They bear thy token proudly on their crest.

## Spanish America

The spirit of the people who built the Escorial still lives throughout a great part of the world in speech, art and social traditions. From the southern tip of South America to Oregon, from San Francisco to Santa Fe, from the Philippines to the Canary Islands, the names of Spain survive. The Romans called their colony Hispania; the flagstone roads of the chariots, aqueducts, and the speech of Rome remain to this day.

The word "Spain" resurrects from the tomb of memory such names as Columbus, Don Quixote with Sancho Panza, Bishop Las Casas, Lope de Vega, Calderon, El Greco, the Cid, Ribera, Velasquez, and Murillo. This was the land of St. Ignatius of Loyola, of Monserrat, St. Teresa of Avila, of sherry wine from Jerez and St. Dominic. This is also the land of the Alhambra, the Alcazar, the shrine of Compostela, and bullfights.

Thanks to Padre Junipero Serra, President of the California Mission Plan, we cannot fail to see the architecture of the Iberian peninsula in the tile-roof Missions. The beautiful Ferry building of San Francisco is the Giralda bell tower of Seville.

The name San Lorenzo still lives not only in California but throughout the world, where countless cities, rivers and mountains are canonized by San and Santa. Because the faith is everlasting, the idea of sanctity will remain in languages til the end of speech, like Trinidad, Los Angeles, and Sacramento.

أَرْضِ وَلَيْسَ لَهُ مِن دُونِهِ أَوْلِيَآءُ أُولَٰٓئِكَ

مَلِّلٍ مُّبِينٍ ۝

أَوَلَمْ يَرَوْا أَنَّ ٱللَّهَ ٱلَّذِي خَلَقَ ٱلسَّمَٰوَٰتِ وَٱلْأَرْضَ

وَلَمْ يَعْىَ بِخَلْقِهِنَّ بِقَٰدِرٍ عَلَىٰٓ أَن يُحْيِۦَ ٱلْمَوْتَىٰ

بَلَىٰٓ إِنَّهُۥ عَلَىٰ كُلِّ شَىْءٍ قَدِيرٌ ۝

وَيَوْمَ يُعْرَضُ ٱلَّذِينَ كَفَرُوا۟ عَلَى ٱلنَّارِ أَلَيْسَ

هَٰذَا بِٱلْحَقِّ قَالُوا۟ بَلَىٰ وَرَبِّنَا قَالَ فَذُوقُوا۟

ٱلْعَذَابَ بِمَا كُنتُمْ تَكْفُرُونَ ۝

بَرَكَاتٍ بَرَأُوا۟ ٱلْأَرْضَ مِنَ ٱلرُّسُلِ وَ

# Mecca to Fatima

There is a special date for the annual pilgrimage to Mecca. In order to protect pilgrims the eleventh month is inviolable; all warfare is suspended. The holy city of Islam is about 45 miles from the Red Sea, resting in a group of hills.

The Koran tells us that Mecca lies in a sterile valley. It became the focus for the caravan trade of the desert. Long before Mohammed, this town was on the incense route as a commercial center and privileged holy place. The territory around the city was known as Haram, "sanctuary"; it was a place of pilgrimage and annual religious fairs.

The citizens of Mecca took the lead in Arabian trade; their hospitality attracted many Bedouins. In the market place might be bought many images. Christianity had reached Mecca, and in the collection could be seen the images of the Virgin and the Child Jesus.

> O Mother, beautiful and mild,
> Enfolding in one sweet embrace
> Your Saviour and your Child.

In the year 622 A.D. a man named Mohammed fled from Mecca to Medina. He was a man who practiced prayer and fasting; he was subject to epileptic fits. When he was 40 years old this prophet claimed that he had received a message from the Archangel Gabriel.

## The Black Stone

At Medina he conquered several tribes and returned in triumph to Mecca. The chief sanctuary was known as Kaaba; it was a stone building without windows, having a door seven feet from the ground.

Teaching that there is one Lord God, Allah, the prophet destroyed all of the images in the sanctuary. The temple was preserved because of the tradition that it had been built by Abraham, the Jewish patriarch, worshipper of the true God.

The chief object of veneration was a black stone among the many idols. Mohammed left the cubical stone on the presumption that it had been given by the Archangel Gabriel to Abraham. This black meteoric rock was fixed at a height so that is could be easily kissed.

At the age of twenty-five Mohammed had married a rich widow who bore him six children. Only Fatima his daughter lived to adult age. The Fatimid dynasty ruled in portions of northern Africa from 909 to 1171.

## Closing the Crescent

Others, besides the descendants of Fatima, claimed the title of Caliph, as successors of Mohammed. They took Jerusalem in 638 and in 717 appeared before Constantinople. They crossed northern Africa and straddled the Gates of Gibraltar. They overran the area of Portugal and Spain, so that the horns of the crescent east and west were about to round to the full.

When Charles, The Hammer, gave a hard blow to the Mohammedans at the battle of Tours in France, the crescent began to wane. But to this day, a small place in Portugal is called Fatima, after the beloved daughter of the Prophet.

Two kinds of pilgrimage revolved around Mecca. There is the omra, or vow of pilgrimage, which is carried out at any opportune moment. There is the haji or annual festive pilgrimage.

The pilgrim reaches the Haram, or sacred territory, with the scanty dress of two cloths wound around his person. He enters the great mosque and makes the sevenfold circuit of the sanctuary. He kisses the black stone of the Kaaba. He then shaves his head and puts on his ordinary dress.

Some of the ceremony is neglected by the pilgrims, but no one misses the "stand" at Arafa. This is a small Hill of Mercy, two or three hours distance from Mecca.

The prayer of pilgrims is always profitable. But the Black Stone of Kaaba is not a gift of the Archangel Gabriel.

> Wings for angels, but feet for men!
> We may borrow the wings to find the way —

We may hope, and resolve, and aspire, and pray,
But our feet must rise, or we fall again.

Only in dreams is a ladder thrown
From the weary earth to the heavenly walls.
But the dream departs, and the vision falls,
And the sleeper wakes on his pillow of stone.
— Josiah Holland.

## Harems and Hammers

Mohammed did nothing to raise the status of women. He pictured heaven as a place where a man had 80,000 servants and 72 wives. His creed shut females up in harems, preached polygamy and doubted the equality of woman's soul with man. The Koran considers slavery a practical necessity.

This bearded prophet set out to conquer the world, cutting down all opposition with the sickle of force. It was Mary who stopped him on the sea at Lepanto.

Don John pounding from the slaughter-painted poop,
Purpling all the ocean like a bloody pirate's sloop,
Scarlet running over on the silvers and the golds,
Breaking of the hatches up and bursting of the holds,
Thronging of the thousands up that labor under sea,
White for bliss and blind for sun and stunned for liberty.
Don John of Austria
Has set his people free!
— G. K. Chesterton

There must have been more smiles in heaven when the same Virgin Mother decided to step to the earth once more, in a place named after Mohammed's daughter.

She chose Portugal, the land of Lisbon and the beautiful Tagus River. Belem and Jeronimos mark the port of Prince Henry the Navigator, Vasco da Gama and Bartolomeu Dias. This is the country of the poet Luis de Camoes, of the ancient university of Coimbra, port wine and Pena castle, fado music and Estorile. Mary returned to the abbey of Alcobaca and Batalha, to Nazare named after her own home town, with the bacalhau, cod fish, sardines and tuna. The faith in her Divine Son is found not only in the Mother country, but also in Madeira, Cape Verde, the Azores, Angola and Mozambique of Africa, Goa, Timor and Macau of the far east. A majestic statue of Christ the King looks over the harbor of Lisbon towards the shrine of Fatima.

There are wrinkles on the face of Mother Earth, because of a warning that another sickle and Russian hammer may almost enslave the earth. But as there was Charles, The Hammer at Tours, so there are countless Fatimites fulminating with the rattle of Rosary beads.

Bernauer Straße

*An Der Mauer*

# Story in Stones

The cathedral of Cologne, in Germany, has celebrated its seventh centenary. The cornerstone was laid on August 14, 1248. There is an old legend about the architect, who bargained his soul with the devil. He offered this price in exchange for the plan of a beautiful edifice. But as soon as the sly builder had the plans, he drove off the devil by confronting Satan with a piece of the true Cross. The damned angel, having been tricked, cried out, "Your name will be unknown and your work will never be finished."

By the time the sanctuary, nave and one tower had been completed it was already 1447. Then for 400 years no further work was added. It seemed that the power of evil had bewitched the structure.

> 'But 'tis strange; And oftentimes, to win
>         us to our harm,
> The instruments of darkness tell us truths,
> Win us with honest trifles, to betray us
> In deepest consequence.
>                 (Macbeth)

However, in 1823 there came a new interest and within 40 years, on October 15, 1880, the Cathedral of Cologne stood finished.

## The Gothic Gift

The first cathedral was the house of some Roman citizen. It was a rectangular building, divided by columns into three aisles, the central one the largest. The master of the house sat at the end of the apse, or bema. The more elaborate homes were called basilicas, or kingly.

The first Christian services were held in private homes, where the bishop presided from a cathedra, a chair. Later when structures were erected for the Holy Sacrifice of the Mass, they were often called basilicas or cathedrals.

The platform on which the table of sacrifice was located was called "the high place," the altar. As the assembly grew in numbers the rectangle near the altar was extended by additional arms. These transepts, in a practical way, provided for the crowd and likewise added the symbol of a cross to the ground plan of the cruciform church.

The Cologne Cathedral belongs to Gothic architecture. This is a loose term which designates that type developed from Romanesque during the 12th century. It is characterized by the pointed arch, ribbed vaults, buttresses and gables of decorative importance.

The nave of the cathedral is 445 ft. long, with 5 aisles. The transepts, with 3 aisles, measure 282 ft. The twin towers lift their stony fingers in prayer at 515 ft.

## Three Wise Heads

Within the cathedral is the shrine of The Three Kings. This reliquary of the Magi is one of the best examples of the goldsmith's art in all the world. The facade of the shrine has three panels. The relief depicts the Virgin with the child Jesus. On the left is a representation of the three kings and Emperor Otto IV. To the right is the scene of the baptism of Christ in the Jordan. The upper portion shows Our Lord enthroned with the archangels Gabriel and Raphael. The sides of the reliquary are sculptured with figures of the Old Testament prophets.

Story says that the relics of the Wise Men were discovered in Persia. It is said that St. Helen brought the remains to Constantinople, whence they were carried to Milan. In 1163 Frederick Barbarossa transferred the relics to Cologne. The shrine contains skulls crowned with jeweled diadems.

> The kings of the earth are men of might,
> And cities are burned for their delight,
> And the skies rain death in the silent night,
> And the hills belch death all day!
> But the King of Heaven, Who made them all,

Is fair, and gentle, and very small;
He lies in the straw, by the oxen's stall.
— Henry W. Longfellow

The grotesque figures, called gargoyles, sitting on the cornice moulding of the cathedral, never dreamed of danger to the edifice from the air. In 1942 their mouths were split wide open with detonating astonishment, when 1,000 airplanes came over Cologne. Nearby was the railroad station and the Hohenzollern Bridge. Cologne was ruined, but the Dom, as the Germans call the Cathedral, was not leveled.

The roof was destroyed and extensive damage was inflicted, but the walls and chapels remained. The reliquary of the Wise Men, who followed the star to the Babe of Peace, escaped the falling comets of war.

## Rock of Ages

The 700th centenary of a cathedral impresses upon us the brevity of one man's life. Even cathedrals will crumble with time, but the faith which built them is eternal. Civilizations are only as strong as the moral fibre of the citizens. We now have cause to worry because builders have lost the soul of society.

The faith that built the Cathedral of Cologne has been vibrant in Germany since the days of St. Boniface and the Christmas tree. It is found in pilgrimages of St. Bartholoma on the Konigsee, in the monasteries of Maria Laach and Weltenburg on the Danube. This land of the Black Forest, the Pied Piper of Hamelin, Munich Beer and Dresden china, the Saar and the Ruhr, the Rhine and the Elbe, cuckoo clocks and violins, will be militant in the faith when the iron curtain has corroded, and the infamous Berlin wall has crumbled.

Throughout the city runs a solid wall,
It separates the Germans, East and West,
It separates the Christians one and all,
It separates the family from the rest.

It separates a mother from her sons,
It separates a father from his girls,
It separates by wires, dogs, and guns,
It separates all flags which freedom furls.

It separates a bishop from his flock,
It separates the sheep and shepherds' call,
The hammer, sickle, stones, all mankind mock
Til tears may wash away the evil wall.

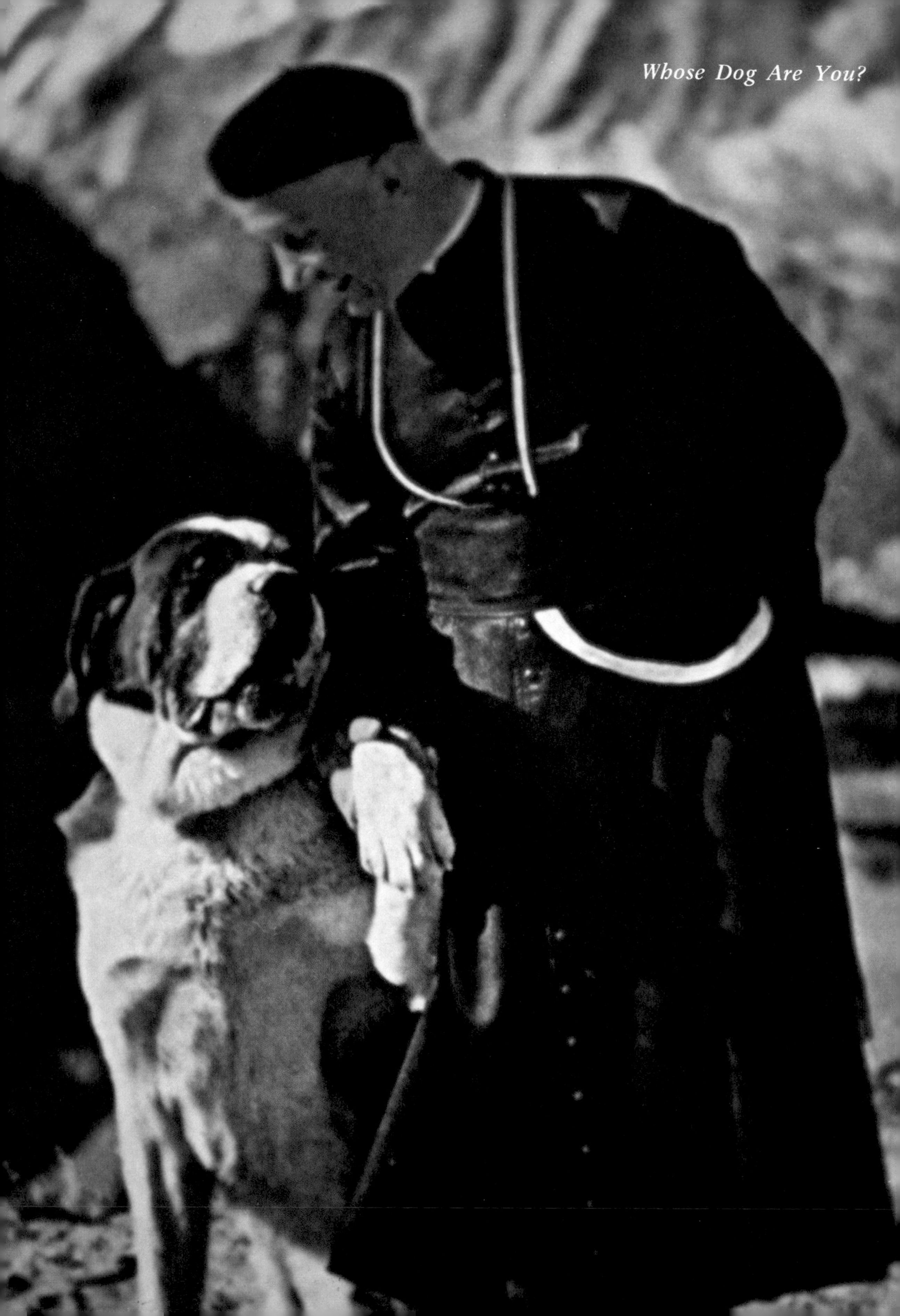

# The Swiss St. Bernard

The dog family is as old as human literature. While walking about the ruins of Pompeii, unearthed from volcanic ashes, the tourist notices an inscription on the stone doorstep. It reads "Cave Canem," "Beware of the dog." The book of Tobias in the Old Testament describes the wagging tail of man's friend.

In some place the domesticated dog separated from the family of the wolf and the jackal. There are, however, so many breeds that no classification can stand unchallenged. One well known, ancient group is the mastiff, which is pictured on the monuments of Babylon. The greyhound group is described in the ancient Egyptian monuments.

From the greyhound and the mastiff came the great dane, the German boarhound. This animal had the speed of the hound and the muscle of the mastiff. When a rough-coated sheepdog met the German boarhound, the original St. Bernard dog was born. The modern mountain dog probably has a strain of Pyrenean or Newfoundland in its breed.

> I am his Highness' dog at Kew;
> Pray tell me, sir, whose dog are you.
> (On a Dog Collar)

## Over the Hump

The St. Bernard is always associated with the great range of mountains in Europe known as the Alps. There are two passes over these peaks; they are called the Great and the Little St. Bernard.

The Little Pass is 39 miles long and reaches an altitude of 7179 feet. The Great Pass leads 53 miles from the Rhone valley of Switzerland into Italy, with a summit of 8111 feet. These crossings were known in Roman times. A temple of Jupiter has been excavated at the top, with votive tablets which belong to the time of Tiberius.

The Romans called the Little Pass the Graia Alps, because of the legend of Hercules. Among the twelve tasks assigned to this strong man was one of bringing the cattle of Graia from Spain to Greece. He not only set up the Pillars of Hercules at the Strait of Gibraltar, but he drove the oxen back through the Alps.

It is said that Hannibal came over the lesser pass on elephants. But the Great St. Bernard Pass was to become famous neither because of the cattle of Hercules nor the elephants of Hannibal. It was a dog that took its very name from the mountains.

> Let Hercules himself do what he may,
> The cat will mew and dog will have his day.
> — Hamlet.

## Brandy and Honey

Most Catholics think that the dog with the brandy barrel is named after the great St. Bernard of Clairvaux, the Frenchman. This Bernard was the second founder of the Cistercian Order, of which the Trappist is the best known branch. He preached the second Crusade, which gave him the nickname of "mellifluous Doctor" — honey mouth.

Bernard was such a good speaker that he talked 31 men into his monastery at Clear Valley, including his father, five brothers and an uncle. He told his smallest brother to stay home, but the youngster replied: "You then take heaven and leave me only earth. The division is too unequal." The only girl in the family entered a Benedictine convent.

You can recognize this St. Bernard in art; he is represented with three mitres on a book, or at his feet. These recall the three time when he refused the bishop's hat. The writings of Bernard on the Blessed Virgin and the Holy Name have been added to the Divine Office.

> Nor voice can sing, nor heart can frame,
> Nor can the memory find,
> A sweeter sound than Thy blest Name,
> O Saviour of mankind.
>
> Jesu, our only joy be Thou,
> As. Thou our prize wilt be;
> Jesu, be Thou our glory now,
> And through eternity.

But the sad-eyed dog of the Alps takes its name from another saint, Bernard of Menthon. This man was born into a very wealthy family, which had planned an honorable marriage for him. He, however, decided to devote his life to the service of the Church and was ordained a priest in 966.

## Road to Rome

For forty-two years he spent himself in teaching the mountaineers and became known as the "Apostle of the Alps." Frequently pilgrims from France and Germany had to take this route to Rome.

For the protection of these pilgrims, St. Bernard built a monastery in the year 962 at the altitude of 8,000 feet. A few years later he established a similar hospice on the Graian Alps, at the Little Pass on the 7,076 foot level.

Thus these two monasteries of the mountains were named St. Bernard. Throughout the centuries the heroic monks have developed well-trained dogs, really without brandy, for aiding travelers lost in the snows. The ski was introduced into Switzerland in 1883 by the same monks.

Ski, auto, and trains have deprived the mountain dog of his heroic task. The dogs of St. Bernard have almost passed into history with Hannibal, Julius Caesar, Charlemagne, Napoleon and others who braved the Alps.

Switzerland is famous for much — such as the Matterhorn, the Jungfrau, clocks and watches, four languages, hydroelectric power, chocolate, cheese and William Tell, the alpenhorn and the Salve Regina at Einsiedeln.

But the sanctity of St. Bernard, the faithfulness of his mountain mastiffs, are as enduring as the everlasting hills. Every man must climb The Seven Storey Mountain.

> The eternal snows appear already past,
> And the first clouds and mountains seem the last;
> But, those attained, we tremble to survey
> The growing labors of the lengthened way,
> The increasing prospects tires our wandering eyes,
> Hills peep o'er hills, and Alps on Alps arise.
> — Alexander Pope

# The Coliseum

One day, in Rome, two tigers smashed out of a circus cage and wandered around the Coliseum. They were finally captured after one had killed a donkey and ripped a large gash in the neck of a circus pony.

Many centuries have passed since wild animals amused some 50,000 people in that amphitheater of Flavian. On that day two animals made crowds run through the streets of the Holy City.

> In vain the surge's angry shock,
> In vain the drifting sands;
> Unharmed, upon the Eternal Rock,
> The Eternal City stands.
> — Samuel Johnson

The circus of Flavian became known as the Coliseum because of its colossal size.

## The Circus

The structure was started by Vespasian and inaugurated by Titus some eight years later in 80 A.D. It is said that this ceremony lasted for 100 days and that during the show 5000 wild animals were killed.

The bowl lies in a depression between the Caelian, the Palatine, and Esquiline hills. The ellipse is 790 feet in circumference, with a length of 620 feet and a width of 525.

45

The upper story was originally of wood, but after a fire in 217 A.D. the entire building was finished in stone.

The height of the four levels reaches 157 feet, and each story represents a different style of architecture. The first has 24 rows ornamented in Doric beauty, the second has 13 rows of Ionic, and the third is embellished with 10 rows of Corinthian architecture. The fourth addition was the work of Alexander Severus and is of composite style.

> To the glory that was Greece,
> And the grandeur that was Rome.

The exterior facade is of travertine and was never covered entirely with marble. The top cornice had apertures for pine masts, from which was suspended an awning to shade spectators.

## The Arena

The arena itself measures 282 feet by 177. Corridors from cages allowed wild beasts to enter the circus. Water conduits made it possible to flood the arena and simulate naval battles.

For 300 years this arena was the scene of gladiatorial fights. In later years the Coliseum was used as a fortress, or arena for bull fights.

In time the huge amphitheater was equivalent to a quarry whence stone was hauled away to be used in the building of churches and palaces.

In the 16th century when some pilgrims asked St. Pius V for relics, he is supposed to have told them to take home some sand from the arena of the Coliseum. Historical investigation, however, seems to indicate that the Coliseum was not the place where most of the early Christians were martyred.

Nevertheless, a cross in the arena and the stations, erected by St. Leonard, give testimony to the many martyrs buried in the catacombs of the Eternal City.

> But stay! these wall — these ivy-clad arcades —
> These vague entablatures — this crumbling frieze —
> These shattered cornices — this wreck — this ruin —
> These stones — alas! these gray stones, are they all,
> All of the famed, and the colossal left
> By the corrosive hours of fate and me?
> — Edgar Poe.

St. Bede had written many centuries ago concerning the Flavian amphitheater:

While stands the Coliseum, Rome shall stand;
When falls the Coliseum, Rome shall fall;
And when Rome falls — the world.

St. Benedict Joseph Labre spent many years in pilgrimages to the principal shrines of Europe. During his last years he lived in the ruins of the Coliseum.

## Faithful Gladiators

Since time grinds down all things, even the stubborn flint, the Coliseum may one day be reduced to dust. But there will be other amphitheaters. At the shrine of the North American martyrs in New York, there is a church modeled after the amphitheater and also called the Coliseum.

Therefore, when a Bishop vests for Holy Mass, he puts on his pectoral cross with these words: "Grant me, Thy unworthy servant, that as I carry this cross containing the relics of Thy saints before my breast, so may I always retain the memory of the passion and victories of Thy holy martyrs."

This pinch of bone is hallowed by a war
Whose battle I can dream of, having known
Something of skirmish and alarms and rout
In my own flesh.
— Alice Clear

The natural beauties of Italy are Naples Bay with Vesuvius, the Amalfi Drive, Capri and the Blue Grotto, Carrara marble, the lakes and mountains of the north with the Dolomites. This is the classical land of the Forum, of Virgil, Cicero, Horace, Livy, Ovid and Tacitus. Here is the genius of Michelangelo, Bernini, Raphael, Titian and Leonardo da Vinci. It is Florence and Dante, Venice the queen of the Adriatic, the Grand Canal and palaces. This is the country of music, the operas of Donizetti, Puccini and Verdi, and bocci ball. Indeed the very vocabulary of music is Italian. This is the birthplace of Caesar and saints, of many Sovereign Pontiffs, of St. Francis, St. Thomas Aquinas and St. Pius X.

*"No Loss of Life"* (Acts XXVII:34)

# The Shipwreck

Many years have passed since St. Paul was wrecked on the island of Malta. An eyewitness, named Luke, a medical man, describes it thus: "As neither sun nor stars were visible for many days and no small storm was raging, all hope of our being saved was in consequence given up.

"Paul got up in the midst of them and said: 'Be of good cheer, for there will be no loss of life, but only of the ship. For last night an angel of the God I belong to and serve stood by me, saying, 'Do not be afraid, Paul, thou must stand before Caesar and God has granted thee all that are sailing with thee.'

"And they ran the ship aground. The prow stuck fast, but the stern began to break up under the violence of the sea. The centurion ordered those who could swim to jump overboard and they brought the rest in, some on planks and others on various pieces from the ship. And so it came to pass that all got safely to land."

Both before and after Paul's shipwreck the islands of Malta have been stepping stones in the march of history between Europe and Africa. The language is an ancient Semitic tongue, related to the Phoenicians who gave us our alphabet.

## Island Fortress

Under the Romans and Cicero, it was called the land of "honey and roses." The Arabs and the Normans, the French and the Spanish, all controlled this island fortress at various times.

For more than two centuries it was the headquarters of knights. When the Crusaders had taken Jerusalem, there developed a brotherhood of men who vowed to take care of sick pilgrims in the Holy Places. These were the knights of St. John.

In time the Hospitallers assumed also military atmosphere, and they went down to defeat with the Crusaders in 1291. They withdrew to the island of Rhodes where they held out until 1522, when the Turks captured it, after a prolonged siege. A few years later the Emperor Charles V gave the Maltese islands to the Order.

> A prince can make a belted night
> A marquis, duke, and a' that;
> But an honest man's aboon his might
> Guid faith, he mauna fa' that.
> — Robert Burns

Malta has been famous for many defensive actions in history. The Knights of St. John held it with less than 2000 men against 40,000 Mohammedans, who finally had to abandon the siege. In the last war this unsinkable battleship was the object of several thousand bombings by Italian and German planes.

This haven of the British Mediterranean fleet was awarded the George Cross. The king's citation embraced all of Malta's 270,000 people for "a heroism and devotion that will long be famous in history."

## The Maltese Cross

During war the Maltese Cross is also prominent on the left sleeve of cadet-nurses. This silver cross, mounted on regimental red, was the symbol of the Knights-Hospitallers during the First Crusade, 1099. The eight points of the Maltese Cross preach again one of the greatest talks of all time, the Sermon on the Mount. No one ever said more in eight sentences than Jesus Christ, the Son of God.

> "How blest are the poor in spirit: the reign of God is theirs.
> Blest too are the sorrowing; they shall be consoled.
> [Blest are the lowly; they shall inherit the land.]
> Blest are they who hunger and thirst for holiness;
>         they shall have their fill.
> Blest are they who show mercy; mercy shall be theirs.
> Blest are the single-hearted for they shall see God.
> Blest too the peacemakers; they shall be called sons of God.
> Blest are those persecuted for holiness' sake;
>         the reign of God is theirs."

## Knights of Malta

Historical descendants of this grand tradition, the Knights of Malta today operate under a new constitution effective January 1, 1957. The Order is now subject to the Holy See, the Vatican Secretariat of State, and the Congregation of Religious.

There are three classifications of Knights of Malta: Religious, with vows of poverty, chastity and obedience, are called Knights of the Just. Those of noble lineage are Knights of Honor and Devotion. Others are known as Knights of Magistral Grace.

Outstanding laymen of the Church, now honored as Knights of Malta, are devoted to the support of hospitals and charitable works. In 1958 the Order set up an international center in Switzerland to study the diseases of leprosy and render aid to its victims.

> How'er it be, it seems to me,
>     'Tis only noble to be good.
> Kind hearts are more than coronets,
>     And simple faith than Norman blood.
>
> —Lord Tennyson

ΓΝΩΘΙ ΣΕΑΥΤΟΝ

# You Speak Greek

With the exception of the Jewish Holy Land, which produced Jesus, the Messiah and Son of God, no small territory ever gave more to civilization than Greece.

Americans begin speaking Greek when they first say "Mama" and "Papa." When the grammar school pupil learns to pronounce "ph" as "f", he has recognized the foreign words, such as "phonograph," "phrase," "hydrophobia."

When he has cut his teeth on "ch" with the sound of "k," he has learned many more Greek words, like "chorus," "character," "Holy Eucharist," "chord," "Christian." The college student begins to think he is educated when he can hiss the letter "Psi." He sometimes forgets that this prefix means the soul in "psychology," "psychosis," "psychic," and "psychasthenia."

## Sport Page

These big words lead us to consider a more intelligible vocabulary, the sport page. We balance the sporting paper against the sugar bowl, only to find that in athletics the Greeks had words for them. The very noun paper smells of the Aegean Sea.

Some columnist informs us that the baseball teams are practicing in a "stadium." "Spheroids" are all over the diamond. Fat *athletes* run several *kilometres,* but few ballplayers could qualify for the *pentathlon.* Their only interest is the *pentagon."* Nearly every noun in this description

53

of spring training is Greek. Of course the Olympic Games were born in the shadow of Mt. Olympus. The *marathon*, a foot race of 26 miles, 385 yards, was inaugurated by Pheidippides, who ran 150 miles for help, fought the battle of Marathon and then raced into Athens to announce the victory. Unfortunately he dropped dead.

Athletics can be overdone. Many a man gets sufficient exercise acting as pallbearer for his friends who take exercise. Some of us feel that the Church Militant, builded on Peter and the Pope, is beginning to shake, when our rooting section feels like giving the "Bronx cheer" to its Catholic team.

The Olympic Games were religious festivals to honor God; the prize was a wreath of wild olive leaves, nothing more. A game is only intended to develop or relax the body, that the soul may more easily hasten towards its goal.

> O God, help me to win;
> But if, in Thy inscrutable wisdom,
> Thou willest me not to win,
> O Lord, make me a good loser.

## Dramatic Critic

If we turn from the sport page to the dramatic columns we are reminded that we owe the stage entirely to the Greeks. The critic writes: "In the theatre today we witnessed *drama*, with *scenes* of *comedy* and *tragedy* intermingled. There were *episodes* of *pathos* and *catastrophe*. There was an excellent *prologue*. The *dialogue* was good also, but I see no reason for the *epilogue*. The play had everything but a Greek *chorus*." There are at least twelve Greek words in this passage and the very word "critic" means a judge.

The vocabulary of the stage, which is Greek, reminds us that indeed all the world's a stage. We are living at the curtain-drop of an era, a turning point in history.

> Act I — this earth, a stage so gloom'd with woe
> You all but sicken at the shifting scenes
> And yet be patient. Our Playwright may show
> In some fifth act what this wild drama means.

Every branch of knowledge uses Greek etymology. The very language of thought is of the Mediterranean. This penetration is found in a random list of words like theory, mathematics, astronomy, philosophy, axiom, hypothesis, logic, barometer and thermometer.

Even our clipped off words are often descended from Homer, whose memory we honor with "auto," "phone," "pep," "steno." The

54

latest jawbreaking terms are of Greek parentage — "bio-chemistry," "genetics," "chemotherapy," "aeronautics," "astronauts."

## Politics and Citizens

Perhaps our greatest debt to the Greeks is their contribution to citizenship. The cause of freedom, the growth of democracy from Greece to Europe, to America, is told in the Greek words of any civics textbook. Monarchy, aristocracy, oligarchy, plutocracy, democracy, ostracism are all words from Greek thought.

This little country invented the names "tyrant" and "despot" long before the current attack of Russia. One who had a care for his rights was called a politician; one not interested in his country was known as an idiotes, — idiot.

Certain it is that if the western world does not speak Greek, it surely thinks Greek.

The little land of Greece gave the world the poetry and drama of Homer, Sappho, Aeschylus, Aristophanes, Sophocles and Euripides, — the philosophy of Diogenes, Socrates, Plato and Aristotle, — the history of Xenophone, Herodotus, Thucydides, and Plutarch, — the glory of Marathon, Thermopylae, and Phidias. In this tongue wrote the great Greek Fathers of the Church — St. John Chrysostom, St. Basil, St. Gregory and St. Athanasius.

Thucydides said, "For we are lovers of the beautiful yet simple in our tastes. And we cultivate the mind without loss of manliness."

From Alexander the Great, Pericles, Hippocrates and Euclid to St. Paul, who preached before the Areopagites on the Hill of Mars, not far from the glorious Parthenon — it may be said

> But Greece and her foundations
> Built below the tide of war,
> Based on the crystalline sea
> Of thought and its eternity;
> Her citizens, imperial spirits,
> Rule the present from the past;
> On all this world of men inherits
> Their seal is set.
> — Shelley

# On the Beautiful Blue Danube

## An der schönen blauen Donau

Johann Strauss. Op. 314

Waltz.

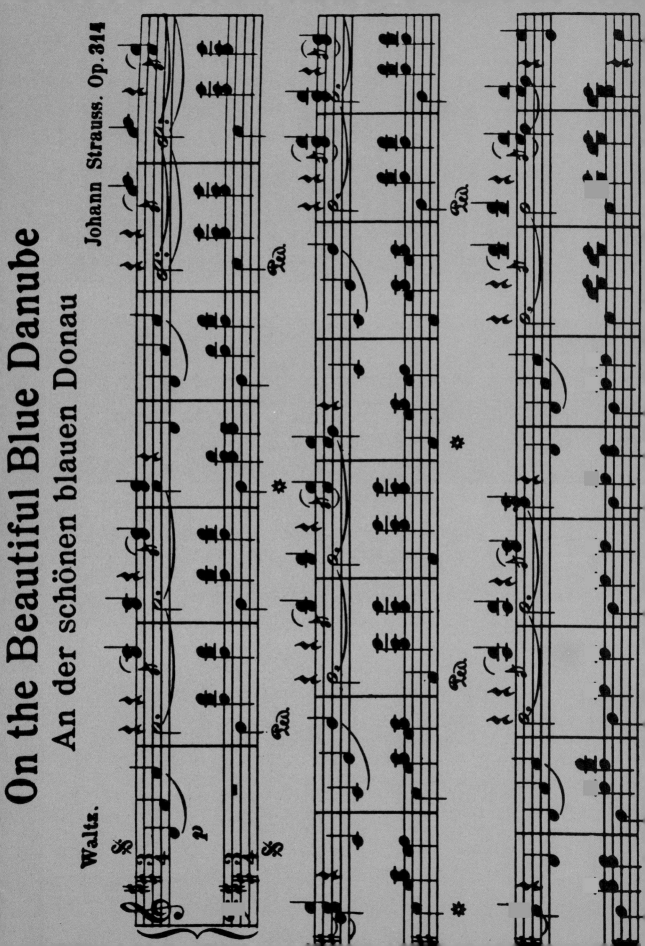

# By the Blue Danube

The Danube is one of the important rivers of the world. It is 1750 miles long and is fed by 300 tributaries. If the waters could speak as they flow along, they might tell of a thousand years during which the crown of St. Stephen has been associated with the Hungarian Magyars.

> Our boat kept measure with its oar.
> The music rose in snatches
> From peasants dancing on the shore
> With boisterous songs and catches.
> Oh, never never
> Can I forget the songs
> Upon the Danube River.

The Communists are not interested in the economic value of the crown. Constructed of iron, it is not worth much more than a few horseshoes. It has not the intrinsic worth of the English jewels — the three crowns of St. Edward, of India and the Imperial State Crown. Why should an uncomfortable piece of iron have any interest to Communists?

## The Iron Crown

Perhaps the atheistic leaders have been suddenly touched by the religious relic of a saintly king. Here is the story of Stephen.

At the close of the ninth century the Magyars came into Hungary. Their language associates them with the Finns and the Ural Mountains. They first came into contact with Christianity through raiding parties into Italy and France.

Their ruler, Geza, seeing the advantage of Christianity, married Adelaide, sister of a Polish duke. Through their influence St. Adalbert of Prague preached the faith in Hungary. When Geza embraced the Catholic religion, his ten year old son, Stephen, was baptized with him.

When he was twenty years old, Stephen married Gisela, sister of the Emperor St. Henry II. Within two years, Stephen succeeded his father as ruler of all the Magyars. Subsequent years were spent in subduing the pagan opponents of Christian unity. Stephen always went to battle only after prayers, fasting and deeds of charity. A monastery, which still exists on "Holy Hill," reminds us that all combat was done under the invocation of St. George and St. Martin.

> My crown is in my heart, not on my head;
> Not decked with diamonds and Indian stones.
> Nor to be seen; my crown is called content;
> A crown it is that seldom kings enjoy.
> — Shakespeare.

Stephen felt that for the glory of God and the good of his people, he should assume the title of King. For this purpose he sent an ambassador to Rome, asking recognition from the Holy Father. Pope Sylvester II gave a crown to St. Astericus with instructions to bring it back to Stephen.

## Buda And Pest

In the year 1001 Stephen was anointed king. The crown sent by the Pope was fitted into another crown, given to King Geza I by Emperor Michael VII. The king built a church in honor of the Mother of God at Stuhlweissenburg, in which the kings of Hungary were to be crowned and buried.

> Hath she beneath her crown of stars
> Remembrance of the thorns wherewith
> Her people crowned her Son? What scars
> Redder than roses in a wreath
> Doth she wear in a coronal
> Under the lights that rise and fall?
> — Katherine Tynan

This church at Suhlweissenburg had been prepared for the future crowning of Emeric, the only son of St. Stephen. But the boy was buried there before his father, for he was killed while hunting. When informed of his son's death, the king remarked: "God loved him, and so He took him away soon."

King St. Stephen of Hungary died on the feast of The Assumption, at the age of 63, when he was buried beside his son in the Church of the Mother of God. His tomb was the scene of miracles, and by order of Pope Gregory VII his relics were enshrined in the Church of Our Lady of Buda. His chief feast in Hungary is August 20, the occasion of the removal of the relics. But Innocent XI put his feast on September 2, 1686, a day when the Emperor Leopold recovered the city of Buda from the Turks. The right bank of the Danube, with Buda, and the left shore of Pest join, unlike Brooklyn and New York, into Budapest.

## Bridges and Gulyas

The ancient capital of Hungary was Buda, which overlooks the Danube, with its old cathedral of St. Matthias. On the lowland across the river is Pest, originally a city of merchants. Beautiful bridges cross the river joining Budapest. This industrial city produces textile, leather goods, iron and furniture.

Hungarian gulyas is cubed meat, with paprika, red onions, boiled potatoes, tomatoes, caraway seeds and noodles. Hungary gave us not only the famous tokay grape, but the doctor Semmelweis and the Hungarian hussars.

For 1,000 years the crown of St. Stephen has been the symbol of a properly constituted government. It is evident that Communism will never eradicate religion; it has likewise found it difficult to dig up the roots of a people's history. Cardinal Mindszenty, and martyrs, always have a resurrection.

Faith of our Fathers, living still
In spite of dungeon, fire, and sword.
Our Fathers chained in prisons dark
Were still in heart and conscience free.
How sweet would be their children's fate,
If they, like them, could die for thee.
Faith of our Fathers, Holy Faith,
We will be true to thee till death!

Modl Sie Za Nami

# The Black Madonna

The Polish people have donated a shrine to Mission Dolores Basilica, San Francisco, California. It is Our Lady of Czestochowa, sometimes known as the Black Madonna.

The picture is painted on cypress board, which, according to story, served as a table in the home of the Holy Family at Nazareth. It has likewise been said that the painter of the picture was St. Luke the Evangelist.

The picture was discovered by St. Helena, who uncovered the True Cross in Jerusalem. The painting remained in Constantinople for some five centuries. The art is obviously Eastern as is the representation of Our Lady of Perpetual Help.

With the invasion of the Tartars in the 14th century, the picture was taken in custody by Prince Adalbert. At the site of Czestochowa there is a bright hillock of white rock, which was called Jasna Gora, Clermont, or Bright Hill.

## Czestochowa, Jasna Gora

The holy picture was entrusted to the Hermits of St. Paul. This Paul was the first hermit, who spent 90 years in the desert of Egypt. An order of monks, named after the hermit, was founded in Hungary in 1225 and became known as the Paulites.

Today there are only 130 professed members distributed in three monasteries. Through the years they have retained custody of the shrine of Czestochowa.

Very noticeable are two long scars on the face of the Virgin's right cheek. In 1430, the shrine of Jasna Gora was attacked by the Protestant Hussites. While they were galloping off with the spoils, the horses suddenly balked and refused to move.

One of the Hussites slashed the picture of Mary and tossed the desecrated image on to the road. Artists have been unable to obliterate the sacrilegious scars, and that is why the Black Madonna shows another dolor in the Basilica of Mission Dolores, dedicated to the Seven Sorrows.

> O Queen of the Seven Sorrows of grief!
> What holy solace, what blest relief
> To come with our little woes to thee
> Who hast fathomed the deeps of Sorrow's sea!

The shrine of Czestochowa in time became the symbol of Polish love of liberty. In 1620 King Sigismund made the hill of Jasna Gora a fortified citadel.

## Queen of Poland

In 1655 Poland was attacked by 1200 Swedish soldiers, who assaulted the hillock. Incredible as it seems, they were defeated by 160 infantrymen, 50 noblemen, and 68 monks.

Beneath the picture of Mary in Mission Dolores are the words "Queen of the Crown of Poland, Pray for Us." This title was adopted in 1656. When the Turks were threatening all Europe, John III Sobieski gathered his knights at Czestochowa and invoked the aid of the Mother of God.

Europe was saved at Vienna by the Polish soldiers and, in commemoration of the salvation, Pope Innocent XI extended the Feast of the Holy Name of Mary to the entire Western church.

In 1717 Pope Clement XI sent two crowns to Jasna Gora; one was placed on the brow of the Black Madonna, and the other on the head of the Infant Jesus.

There was a sacrilegious theft in 1909 and both crowns disappeared. Fittingly, the crowns which now adorn Mary and the Infant were donated by our Holy Father, St. Pius X.

> You shall restore me, O my last Ally,
> To the vengeance and the glories of the bold.
> This is the faith that I have held and hold,
> And this is that in which I mean to die.
> — H. Belloc

# Mater Dolorosa

The wounds on the face of the Blessed Mother tell also the story of the sufferings of Poland. Pope Pius XII reminded the Poles that a nation, which has so loved Mary, will certainly see a resurrection.

"Your heavenly Patroness and Mother, whose intercession you have been entreating through the centuries with the touching tenderness of loving children, will lead Poland out of darkness and out of the tempest, and bring her finally to the port of peace."

Poland has given to the world the poet and mystic Adam Mickiewicz, and Juliuz Slowacki. Hers is Henryk Sienkiewicz, the author of Quo Vadis, and Joseph Conrad the novelist. The scientists Mr. and Mrs. Pierre Curie came from Poland, as well as Frederic Chopin, creator of immortal mazurkas and polanaises. We are indebted to Poland for both Pulaski and Kudziusko, who assisted in the American Revolution.

Yes the River Vistula, the Carpathian Mountains, Cracow and the Wawel Cathedral have watched the greatness of the people of Poland.

To the Bishops of Poland, Pope Pius XII said: "Turn to the hillock whence aid will come. Let your eyes rest on the summit named by your Fathers Jasna Gora. There the Mother of God and your Queen has established her abode."

> Nigdym ja ciebie, ludu, nic rzucila.
> Nigdym ci mego nie odjela lica,
> Ja po dawnemu, moc twoja i sila
> Bodgarodzica.

С Рождеством
Христовым

# Russian Santa Claus

On December 6, both the Eastern and Western liturgies honor St. Nicholas, Bishop of Myra. His biography is brief. During the persecution of Diocletian he was tortured and imprisoned. It is said that he survived and was present at the Council of Nicea, although this fact is not mentioned by St. Athanasius, the champion of that gathering.

This saint of Christmas first became popular when his body was stolen. Nicholas was born at Patara, in Lycia, Asia Minor. In 1087 some Italian merchants took his relics from Myra to Bari, in Italy. From that time the Bishop became the patron saint of sailors. A common nautical expression is, "May St. Nicholas hold the tiller." In sailor language:

> Unquiet ripples lisp and purr,
> A block there pipes, and chips i' the sheave,
> The wheelropes jar, the roof-points stir
> Faintly — and it is Christmas Eve.
> — John Masefield.

## Bishop Nicholas

From time immemorial Bishop Nicholas has been associated with the charity of gift-giving. In the days when alimony meant "to feed the poor," a lady came to marriage with a dowry. This sum of money was supplied by her father. Since only death broke the bond of love, the dowry was a provision for support, if she became a widow.

The story is told that Nicholas threw three bags of gold into a family window for the dowry of three impoverished maidens. Thus he becomes a symbol of marriage pure as gold, rather than the gold-digging brass of divorcees. To this day the three balls in front of a pawnshop tell the tale of Santa Claus.

The name Santa Claus, however, came to us from a turn of his name through the Dutch. In 1822 Clement C. Moore was riding home on a sleigh, with his friend Jan Duyckinck, a Dutchman. As they moved through the snow Jan entertained his companion with stories about St. Nicholas.

That night, before going to bed, Moore began to scribble on a piece of paper some descriptive verse. On Christmas day the poem was read to the children and then thrown into a desk.

## On Donder, On Blitzen

A year later the children remembered the story and asked for a re-reading. On this occasion a guest gave a copy of the lines to the Sentinel Troy, N.Y. Thus Santa Claus came to the American children on Dec. 23, 1823, when the world read of "A Visit From Saint Nicholas."

> 'Twas the night before Christmas,
>     when all through the house
> Not a creature was stirring, not even a mouse.
> The stockings were hung by the chimney
>     with care,
> In hopes that St. Nicholas soon would be there.

In some countries of Europe it is the custom to elect a boy Santa Claus at Christmas time. In imitation of the Bishop of Bari, the youngster is given a miter and a crozier. He rules his mythical diocese from Dec. 6, the Feast of Bishop Nicholas, until Dec. 28, the day of the Holy Innocents.

St. Nicholas is the patron of Russia. Before the Communistic atheists began their war on Russia's God, some kind of shrine in honor of Bishop Nicholas could be found in every church. His eikon could be seen in every household. The Russian Orthodox Church observes, as a holy day and holiday, the Feast of the Translation.

This is the anniversary of May 9, 1087, when the Italians landed at Bari, with the relics of St. Nicholas, removed out of the hands of the Saracens. Before the haters of God and good, in Russia, began their attack on the Orthodox Church, countless Russians came as pilgrims to Bari. So many were they that the Russian government maintained a hospital and hospice there for the visitors.

But this patron of Russia is known to all the world. Even in the 10th century a Greek wrote: "The West as well as the East acclaims and glorifies him. All Christians, young and old, men and women, boys and girls, reverence his memory. And his favors, which know no limit of time and continue from age to age, are poured out over all the earth."

## Marx and Mary

That Russian minority, the Communists, which is enslaving the nation, has not yet succeeded completely in killing Santa Claus and the Faith. Some day there will be a resurrection, and St. Nicholas will again replace Nicholas Lenin, and St. Joseph will be honored more than Joe Stalin, and Mary will survive Marxism.

There are 15 Soviet Socialist Republics, embracing an area twice the size of the United States. Some 59 nationalities speak about 100 languages. Russia is the literature of Pushkin, Dostoyevsky, and Tolstoi; it is the music of Tchaykovsky, Stravinsky and Rimsky-Korsavkov.

This is the country of the first satellite, Sputnik, and the first man in space, Gagarin. It includes also the fabled city of Samarkand, with Tamerlane's tomb, as well as Yalta. It is Russia, with the Kremlin, the Czar's bell, Red Square, the Bolshoi Theatre, and the ancient St. Basil's Cathedral. It is Leningrad, the Hermitage, the Winter Palace, St. Isaac's and the fountains of Peterhof.

In the meantime St. Nicholas is the harbinger of a birthday, which outlives all tyranny because it is a victory of love, Christmas.

> When, what to my wondering eyes should appear,
> But a miniature sleigh and eight tiny reindeer,
> With a little old driver, so lively and quick
> I knew in a moment it must be St. Nick. . . .
> As I drew in my head, and was turning around,
> Down the chimney St. Nicholas came with a bound. . . .
> But I heard him exclaim, ere he drove out of sight,
> "Happy Christmas to all, and to all a good-night!"

# The Straight Street

January 25 marks the conversion of a man, who was told by a heavenly vision: "Arise and go to the street called Straight." Many cities claim to have the longest, straightest street in the world. Some citizens say it is in Salt Lake; other bus-spielers proclaim San Francisco's Market street both the longest and widest. Some would even say that Mission street runs from the Embarcadero to Mission Dolores and all the way to San Diego.

A bishop, visiting Syria, inquires immediately for Straight street. He is anxious to compare it with Main street in his own home town. He knows that the place is in Damascus, the oldest uninterrupted habitation in the world.

The traveler stops at the outskirts of the city and checks his bearings with a guide book, The Acts of the Apostles, by a physician named Luke. In the Greek of St. Luke, written about A.D. 63, he reads:

"But Saul, still bearing threats of slaughter against the disciples of the Lord, went to the high priest and asked him for letters to the synagogues at Damascus, that if he found any men or women belonging to this Christian Way, he might bring them in bonds to Jerusalem."

## Stephen vs Saul

Near the city of Damascus, a light from heaven shone round him, and falling to the ground, he heard a voice saying to him, "Saul, Saul, why dost thou persecute Me? I am Jesus, whom thou art persecuting." When Saul arose he was blind and his companions led him by the hand into Damascus, where for three days he neither ate nor drank until miraculously cured.

This was the same Saul, who stood by with the garments of Stephen, consenting to the death of the first martyr.

> If Stephen had not prayed at all
> Would the Church have Paul
> In place of Saul?

This description is repeated twice in the words of Paul himself. The apostle describes the scene near Damascus in a discourse delivered in the midst of a mob shouting for his death. Paul said to the tribune of the soldiers: "I am a Jew from Tarsus in Cilicia, a citizen of no insignificant city. But I beg thee, give me leave to speak to the people."

These events, on the way to Damascus, are narrated a third time when Paul stands before King Agrippa. So well does Saul describe his conversion that the king comments: "In a short while thou wouldst persuade me to become a Christian." Paul concludes with a joke: "I would to God everybody would be like I am, excepting of course these chains."

> But though my wing is closely bound,
> My heart's at liberty;
> My prison walls cannot control
> The flight, the freedom of the soul.
>                         — Jeanne Guyon

## Damascus

The city of Damascus lies at the base of the Anti-Lebanon range, in a plain of perhaps 30 miles. The Street called Straight, which Saul was told to find, is about a quarter-mile long, without a bend. The ancient Roman name Vicus Rectus, and the Arab term Derb el Moustaquim both mean Straight street.

This thoroughfare, like many other streets, is covered. The bazaars of Damascus are sidewalk stores, fronting a passageway covered with corrugated iron. Customers jam the middle of the street like a parade. The Arab chauffeur moves along in low gear, butting pedestrians and donkeys to either side like a snow plow.

Damascus is the oasis of the desert, the crossroads of civilizations. Blessed with abundant water from the El Barada river, it blossoms with fruits of every description. So many apricots fill the air with perfume that it has carried all the way to the Iberian peninsula, where both the Spanish and Portuguese word for apricots is "damascos."

For self or others, good or ill,
Life is ordained to bear, like land,
Some fruit, be fallow as it will.
— Richard Milnes.

Caravans of camels used to travel about 25 miles a day, bearing the luxuries of the Orient from Bagdad. Now desert trucks, air-conditioned, drive by compass over the trackless sands with the recklessness that only a religious Arab can exhibit.

## Saladin vs Crusaders

Other great men have walked the Street called Straight. Here was born St. John Damascene, the last of the Greek Fathers. At the end of the Street is the Grand Mosque, once a Christian Church built by the Emperor Theodosius in A.D. 375. Within is the tomb of Saladin, perhaps the most revered character in all the history of this Mohammedan world.

This is the man who drove the Crusaders from the Holy Land, and overcame Richard the Lion-hearted. He destroyed the Latin kingdom with a celebrated victory at the saddle-shaped mountain near Cana of Galilee, known as the Horns of Hattin. When preparing for his own funeral he told his standard bearer to carry a rag on a lance through Damascus, shouting: "At his death, the King of the East could take nothing with him except this cloth."

When the tourist steps from Straight street into the mosque, he reads above the beautiful colored marble of the sarcophagus, the Arabic prayer: "O God, accept this soul, and open to him the gates of Heaven, that last victory for which he hoped." Yes, great men have walked the Street called Straight.

The wisest men are glad to die; no fear
Of death can touch a true philosopher.
Death sets the soul at liberty to fly.

*Exalted as cedars*

# Cedars of Lebanon

Our Mother, the Church, says of the Blessed Virgin: "I was exalted like a cedar tree on Mount Lebanon." These words are in her official prayer of October 7, the feast of the Holy Rosary. They are repeated on October 11, the Maternity of Mary.

Lebanon is today an independent country just north of Palestine. Its coastal plain is a perfumed garden, framed in blue-tinted mountains with dark ravines. Melting snows furnish life to this oasis in the general desert of the Middle East. Farming here has been excellent since the days of the Phoenicians, the inventors of our alphabet.

## Land of Phoenicians

The soil of Lebanon will produce tobacco, cereals, bananas, vineyards, potatoes and all the fruits of California. But the glory of the land has been cedars, cypresses and pines. The national flag of the Lebanese waves an image of the cedar.

The cedar is a cone-bearing tree; its dark evergreen leaves grow in tufts. The branches spread out horizontally and sometimes the spread of the tree is greater than its height.

> Cedar, and pine, and fir
> A sylvan scene, and as the ranks ascend
> Shade above shade, a woody theatre
> Of stateliest view.
> — John Milton

73

These trees do not grow in extensive forests, but rather in separate groves. The visitor from California ascends the mountain of Lebanon, expecting to see trees like an expansive forest of redwood giants. He finds only a few hundred cedars which might astound a citizen of the prairie States, but which seem like bushes to a lumberjack from timber country.

There was a time when the Lebanese mountains were covered with many cedars, but time and the recklessness of invaders have denuded the landscape. The few beautiful surviving cedars are now officially protected by the government. But it is too late to shout:

> Woodman, spare that tree! . . .
> Touch not a single bough!
> In youth it sheltered me,
> And I'll protect it now.
> — George Morris

In arid land any tree is a God-send, greatly appreciated by man. It was natural that the cedars of Lebanon should become a symbol in conversation, and in poetry, for all the people of this Middle East. So popular was the tree that it is mentioned in a fable, even as we might talk of the rabbit and the tortoise. In the biblical Book of Kings we may read: "A thistle of Lebanon said to a cedar tree, which is in Lebanon . . ."

## Solomon's Temple

The cedar was known, first of all, for its beauty. The reddish-white wood gave off a fragrant odor; its timber was sought by Solomon when he planned to build the temple at Jerusalem.

King Solomon sent word to Hiram of the coastal city of Lebanon, called Tyre, presuming on his friendship with David, "Give orders that thy servants cut me down cedar trees of Lebanon and let my servants be with thy servants."

The reply of King Hiram is likewise quoted in the Bible: "I will do all thy desire concerning cedar trees. My servants will bring them down from Lebanon to the sea. I will put them together in floats in the sea, and convey them to the place, which you will signify."

All through the Bible the cedar is extolled for its beauty. It is called "the glory of Lebanon," "most beautiful for the spreading of its branches," "the cedar of God."

The beautiful cedar also became the symbol of a long life, of durability. The fragrant wood contains a resinous oil, which protects it against worms and dry rot. Pieces of the tree have been found in ruins, which have been dated as 2700 years old.

We saw the Tribes as captives led,
We saw them back return anon;
As rafters have our branches dead
Covered the porch of Solomon.
And later, when the Word, made man,
Came down to God's salvation-plan,
To pay for sin the ransom price
The beams that formed the Cross we gave,
These, red in blood of power to save
Were altars of that sacrifice.

               — Alphonse de Lamartine


The size and strength of the cedar were also proverbial. The height of a mature tree, which might come close to 100 ft., prompted the Sacred Writer to observe: "The cedar God has exalted above all the trees of the country."

## The Exalted Tree

Years before the birth of Christ, the prophet called the Messiah and His Church, a cedar tree. "I myself, saith God, will take of the marrow of the high cedar and I will plant it on a mountain high and eminent and all birds shall dwell under it."

When our Mother the Church began to compose Masses and prayers in honor of the Blessed Virgin, she accommodated words of the Old Testament. The cedar was celebrated for its beauty, its durability and majesty. It had been said: "The righteous shall grow like a cedar in Lebanon." Surely then all adjectives descriptive of a good soul apply to Mary Immaculate.

On August 15, a Bishop with an Episcopal motto, "Sursum Corda, Maria Assumpta" offered Mass in the shadows of cedars. Above him was a statue of Our Lady of Lebanon, with the thought:

O Mary, Queen of mountains and seas,
purer than Lebanon snow and flowers,
ever higher like the Lebanon Cedars —
include us in your motherly love.

*"Shema Israel"*

# The Pilgrims' Medal

The word saunter means to walk like a pilgrim ("sainte terre"), to the Holy Land. The modern pilgrim may drop from the skies, with the delightful dew of San Francisco still on his coat, and stand on Mount Scopus. This vantage point has been known as Lookout Hill because one looks down on Jerusalem, as did a long line of invaders and liberators.

This view of the Holy City prompts the memory with the song of David: "I rejoiced at the things that were said to me. We shall go into the House of the Lord. Our feet were standing in thy courts, O Jerusalem."

The city is holy to the Jews, because there was the temple of Solomon. It is holy to the Moslems because they have built a mosque over Solomon's courts and think that from this rock Mohammed went to heaven.

It is holy for Christians because it witnessed much of the life of Jesus, especially the Last Supper, the Passion, Death and Resurrection.

## Mt. Sion

Thus the pilgrim looks on Mt. Sion even as it was seen by the Roman Titus, who destroyed the temple and city, or by the invading Moslems, or the liberating crusaders.

> It is he that saith not "Kismet"; it
>    is he that knows not Fate;
> It is Richard, it is Raymond, it is

Godfrey in the gate!
It is he whose loss is laughter when
he counts the wager worth.
— G. K. Chesterton

Whoever has visited the Holy Land wishes to retain some souvenir of his pilgrimage. For this reason Pope Leo XIII instituted the Cross of Honor. This is a medallion with a likeness of the Sovereign Pontiff and the inscription "Founded by Leo XIII, 1900." The badge is a cross embracing four smaller crosslets, the standard of the Crusaders. Around the arms of the cross are the words: "The Love of Christ Crucified Has Drawn Us."

All the soil of Palestine from Beersheba to Dan is holy land; biblical scenes are recalled from Egypt to Lebanon. The pilgrim's medal has chosen four shrines for representation.

## Nazareth, Bethlehem, Cenacle

There is a picture of Nazareth, where the pilgrim journeyed to witness the place of the Annunciation. It reminds him of the angel Gabriel and the first Hail Mary. When he knelt at the Creed of the Mass and said, "Verbum caro factum est," his eyes read on the ground the words, "the Word Became Flesh."

The second scene is Bethlehem, the town of David, Ruth, and the Shepherds. When the pilgrim-priest stood at the manger and said: "I will go into the altar of God," his eye fell on a silver star and the words: "Here was born Jesus Christ of the Virgin Mary."

Away in a manger, no crib for a bed,
The little Lord Jesus lay down His sweet head,
The stars in the sky looked down where He lay,
The little Lord Jesus asleep in the hay.

A third medallion pictures the Jordan River, where John was baptizing. The visitor recalls the water, flowing by on the way to the Dead Sea, where Sodom and Gomorrah, the cities of sin, were obliterated. At the Jordan's bank a voice was heard: "This is My beloved Son. Hear Him."

The fourth scene chosen for this pilgrim's medal is the Cenacle, the sacred Upper Room, a battlefield between the Arabs and Jews. Here the Master celebrated His Last Supper; here He came after the Resurrection and established the Sacrament of Penance; here on Pentecost, the fiftieth day, the Apostles received the Holy Spirit.

Turning over his Cross of Honor, the traveler reads on the large cross: "A Token of Holy Pilgrimage to Jerusalem." The center scene shows the Resurrection, a fitting memorial of the Basilica of the Holy

Sepulchre. The small medallions are tokens of Christ's humanity. Here is the garden of agony, there the scourging at the pillar. A representation of the crowning with thorns is balanced by a picture of the crucifixion.

Thus the pilgrim carries a lasting memorial of the Garden of Gethsemane and the Hill of Olives. Frequently in memory he walks the Via Dolorosa, winding through the city streets.

## Sauntering

The pilgrim takes leave of the Holy Land, his souvenir medal hanging from a silken red ribbon, with four strips of blue and white margin, intersected by a yellow thread.

His cross contains only nine scenes from his pilgrimage. But his memory retains ninety-nine — indeed the parable of the Good Shepherd, the storm on the Lake of Galilee, and all the gospels.

All of the major shrines were enriched by the Church with an opportunity for a plenary indulgence. Secondary Biblical locations were made the occasion for partial indulgences. Religious objects, which had touched one of the Sanctuaries, acquired the Apostolic Indulgences.

Pope Leo XIII did not want the memory of the Sacred Places to vanish from the pilgrim's life. He added a final indulgence, granted to the person who saunters to the Holy Land and departs with lingering steps. The indulgence was granted for that last look at the Holy City and the song of exile.

> By the streams of Babylon we sat and wept
> when we remembered Zion.
> On the aspens of that land we hung up our harps.
> How could we sing a song of the LORD in a foreign land?
> If I forget you, Jerusalem, may my right hand be
> forgotten!
> May my tongue cleave to my palate if I remember you not,
> If I place not Jerusalem ahead of my joy.

It remained for Pope Paul VI to be the first Pope who returned to the land of Peter, the first Vicar of Christ. All the world watched him on television when he blessed himself with the water of Galilee, and stood at the spot where Jesus said to Peter, "Feed my lambs. Feed my Sheep."

Delenda est Carthago

# The Carthagenian Sea

As we sail here in the moonlight over the Mediterranean Sea we are looking toward Africa. There once stood the great city of Carthage. Virgil has the story in his Aenead. After sailing from Tyre at the other end of the sea, Dido, the queen, had landed at the tip of North Africa.

At Lybia the natives told her that she might purchase as much of their land as she could cover with an ox-hide. Like most ladies, Dido was a good shopper and clever bargainer. She cut up the hide into many small tiny strips, with which she proceeded to measure out the site of the future city of Carthage.

## The Didoes

From the wind-swept plains of dusty Troy Aeneas was blown to Africa, where for one year Dido proposed to him by entertainment of every kind. But Aeneas decided to continue his odyssey; he departed secretly and Dido awoke only to see the last sail crossing the straits to Sicily.

Then Dido had a fit which added the word didoes to the dictionary. Seeming to be angry she collected all the belongings of the sailor into a pile, and on top she placed an image of Aeneas. She set it afire, jumped into the flames and stabbed herself.

> Much have I seen and known; cities of men
> And manners, climates, councils, governments;

81

And drunk delight of battle with my peers,
Far on the ringing plains of windy Troy. — Tennyson.

The second story of Carthage is found in the word Punic. The propaganda of the Romans was so good, or bad, that even the word has been unjustly turned to mean "untrustworthy." Three times Rome and Carthage joined battle in what history calls the Three Punic Wars.

The first was a battle for Sicily. Carthage had the sea-power and used to say that no Roman could wash his hands in the sea without her permission. The consul Regulus was captured and later sent back to Rome as a hostage to sue for peace. Instead of arranging peace, he kept his eyes on the ground in order not to see his wife and child, and told the Romans to keep fighting.

## Delenda est Carthago

The great military genius of Carthage was Hamilcar, nicknamed Barca Lightning, because he was the ancient blitz. When his son Hannibal was 9 years old his father made the boy swear eternal hostility to Rome.

Hannibal performed the incredible task of crossing the Alps and camping before Rome. For generations the Roman mothers used to hush their children to sleep with the warning, "Shush! Hannibal at the gates."

It was another brother, Hasdrubal, who crossed the mountains with 56,000 men and 15 elephants. However, his messenger sent to his brother was captured and the military plans discovered. The Romans deployed their full strength against a divided force and defeated Hasdrubal.

They cut off the general's head and threw it into the camp of his brother. In the words of Livy, Hannibal withdrew "leaving the country of his enemy with more regret than many an exile has in leaving his own."

In the Roman Senate Cato used to rise and hold up a bunch of figs, orating, "These figs grow but three days' sail from Rome. Every speech which I make in this house will finish with "Delenda est Carthago, 'Carthage must be destroyed.' "

Hoping for peace, Carthage in time disarmed herself and the wily Romans burned the noble city. In the custom of the time salt was sown on the soil and the land cursed. Cities like persons come into being, enjoy their youth, reach maturity and die.

Look on my works, ye mighty, and despair!
Nothing beside remains. Round the decay
Of that colossal wreck, boundless and bare
The lone and level sands stretch far away.
— Robert Browning.

## Augustin of Hippo

While we sail along Africa we think of the greatest African of them all, the Bishop of Hippo, St. Augustine. While waiting for a boat to return to Carthage his mother, St. Monica, died near Rome. Her last words were, "Lay this body anywhere. Only be sure to remember me at the altar of God."

In his confessions Augustine meditates on the ruins of Carthage. "I filled my head with the wanderings of Aeneas, while I forgot my own wanderings. I shed tears over the death of Dido, when in the meantime, wretched creature that I was, I passed by with dry eyes myself dying in these things, from Thee, O God, my life.

"For what is more miserable than for one that is in misery to have no commiseration upon himself and to weep for the death of Dido and not to bewail his own death caused by not loving THEE."

> Vainly strives the soul to mingle
> With a being of our kind.
> Vainly heart with our hearts are twined.
> For the deepest still is single.
> An impalpable resistance
> Holds like natures still at distance.
> Mortal! Love that Holy One
> Or dwell for aye alone.
> (Aubrey de Vere)

# Roaming Home

The difference between a tourist and a gypsy is that the former eventually comes home. There are various opinions concerning the starting place of the Romany trail. The Gypsies are met in all the countries of the world.

The word gypsy is an abbreviation of the name Egyptian, which comes from one theory that these people originated in the land of Pharaoh.

Defenders of this opinion even cite the Scripture to indicate that these nomads were dispersed from Egypt. "I will scatter the Egyptians among the nations; and will disperse them through the countries." (Ezech. 29:12).

> Egypt! from whose all dateless tombs arose
> Forgotten Pharaohs from their long repose
> And shook within their pyramids to hear
> A new Cambyses thundering in their ear;
> While the dark shades of forty ages stood
> Like startled giants by Nile's famous flood.
> — Lord Byron

Legends are told that the ancestors of those people refused lodging to the Divine Child, the Virgin Mary and Joseph, when they fled into Egypt from the tyrant Herod.

85

## Egyptian Gypsies

Another guess thinks that the gypsies are of the Semite race. Fable has it that their ancestors stole one of the four nails from the cross of Christ and as punishment were condemned to wander. It is most probable, however, that the gypsies came from India.

One thing certain is the existence of these vagabonds in almost every country of the world.

The gypsy has no national costume, but he distinctly retains his individuality. There is a noted fondness for bright colors, such as green, yellow and red. In America there are about 100,000 on the Romany trail.

From ancient times gypsies were known for their skill as metal smiths. The art of hammering iron and copper is part of their tradition. They were also notorious for their cunning in horse trading. The women of the tribe gathered in money by telling the fortunes, with cards and palmistry, of less intelligent, more educated aristocrats.

## Romany Road

The language, called Romany, is a special dialect, which absorbs certain expressions from the country in which the nomad travels. There is a similarity between Romany and the language of India. There are many Greek words found in the gypsy dialect, which indicates that the people moved from India through Asia Minor and Greece.

The gypsy is well known for his love of music. His favorite instruments are the violin, the cymbal and the lute. His orchestra might contain violins, viola, cello, and a cymbal; at times he might include a clarinet, but never any noisy brass. The Hungarian composer and pianist Franz Liszt wrote:

"What fascinates the listener more than anything else in this music is its rhythmic freedom, wealthy variety, and flexibility, which are not to be found anywhere else to the same degree."

"In the matter of the rhythmic invention and its right employment we know no other source from which European music could so abundantly learn."

The gypsy performs acrobatic feats with a violin. He can balance it on his head or on his back while playing; he can use the bow with his teeth. With the strings he can imitate the canary, the organ, or the nightingale.

Verdi's opera, Il Trovatore, pictures something of the gypsy atmosphere and the popular superstition about the race. The opera also makes capital of the gypsy talent for metal work and horseshoeing, by giving us the well-known anvil chorus. The carefree people dance and sing around the anvils.

See, how the shadows of night are flying!
Morn breaks, heaven's glorious arch unveiling;
Like a young widow, who, weary of sighing,
Lays by her garments of sorrow and wailing.
Rouse up to labor! Take, each his hammer!
Who makes a gypsy's life with pleasure laden?
The gypsy maiden.

The religion of the gypsy, like his life, is somewhat unsettled. It generally follows the country in which he travels and retains certain superstitions of gypsy lore. In family morals he is superior to many who think themselves cultured.

## An Odyssey

The law of the tribe reverences virginity and marital fidelity; children are considered the greatest possession. Perhaps this is why the gypsy has continued to retain his identity through so many centuries, while more powerful nations are becoming historical suicides, by practicing neither birth nor control.

The pyramids of Egypt and the sphinx have been standing still for centuries, but the gypsies move on. The camel can go about 17 days without water, but the gypsies seem always to find an oasis. Feluccas on the Nile were the main mode of transportation for Egypt, the gift of the Nile, but gypsies generally spurn navigation. Egypt produced astronomers, mathematicians, scribes, engineers and farmers, but the gypsy is a true nomad.

Blacks and Whites

# The Dark Continent

The dark continent of Africa is so large and so diversified, influenced by so many colonizers, that the name does not clearly identify it. The common denominator is the color of the inhabitants who outnumber the whites 35 to 1.

For centuries this continent was hardly known to the Europeans, except for Egypt and the land about Carthage. The monumental pyramids of Giza and the temples of Karnak and Luxor tell us of a civilization which was old when Greece was young. Egypt is the land visited by the Divine Infant when Joseph and Mary fled with Him from the tyrant Herod. On the Mediterranean the Phoenician city of Carthage contended with Rome for the inland sea.

## Natal to Kilimanjaro

Perhaps the first European to appreciate the size of Africa was Vasco Da Gama, the devout Portuguese, who sighted a point on Christmas Day in 1497. This he called Natal in honor of the Redeemer's birth.

> Christmas in lands of the fir tree and pine,
> Christmas in lands of the palm tree and vine,
> Christmas where snow peaks stand solemn and white
> Christmas where cornfields lie sunny and bright.
> — Phillips Brooks

Africa abounds in natural wonders from north to south. The Sahara desert is so large that the entire continental United States might be dropped into it. The top of the land is snowcapped Mt. Kilimanjaro at 19,300 feet and Mt. Kenya which scrapes the sky at 17,056 feet. Lake Tanganyika is a freshwater lake 500 miles long, and Lake Victoria is larger than any of the Great Lakes of America, with the exception of Lake Superior.

Victoria Falls are two and a half times higher than Niagara and also much wider. Three great rivers of the world wind their course through the continent under the names Congo, Niger and Nile. The last stream would reach all the way from New York to the North Pole.

Africa is the last refuge for the big game animals. Large sanctuaries, in many countries, protect many animals against their greatest enemy, man.

This is the world of elephants, giraffes and zebras. Here is the habitat of the river-horse, called by the Greeks, hippopotamus, and the crocodile. Here, too, lumbers the horn-nosed beast also with a Greek name, rhinoceros. Lions and leopards, every species of antelope, and buffalo add to a thriving menagerie. Nor should one forget the baboon, the chimpanzee and the gorilla, the swift cheetah, the ostrich and flamingo.

The land also abounds in hillocks of termites, sometimes called erroneously, ants. These mounds of earth are cemented by saliva from the insects, and when mixed with soil they serve to pave secondary roads. The notorious tsetse fly brings sleeping sickness and nagana to man and beast. This African fly is a relative of the stable, the horn, and the common housefly.


## Doctor Livingston, I Presume


It was only about 100 years ago that the first European crossed Africa or visited the heart of the Congo. Henry Morton Stanley was commissioned by his newspaper to find a missionary named David Livingstone. He succeeded with the well-known, but unhistoric greeting, "Dr. Livingstone, I presume?" On a second journey, however, Stanley set out from the east coast and after great danger and hardship reached the estuary of the Congo on the Atlantic side. This was the first real crossing of the dark continent.

Natives of Africa are called by the general name Negro, which means black. However, there are dark skinned people in the tropics all around the world. Pigment is a natural protection against ultraviolet rays of the sun. Not even in Africa are all the colored completely negroid.

# Beautiful and Black

It has been said that three kings have been represented at the Christmas crib to suggest the white, the yellow, and the black race.

> Three kings came riding from far away
> Melchior, Gaspar, and Baltasar
> And their guide was a beautiful, wonderful star.
> — Longfellow

It has likewise been said that the three sons of Noe named Sem, Cham and Japhet are the ancestors of the three races.

One thing, however, is scientifically certain; we are all descended from one father, Adam, and spiritually all Christians are Semites. In her chant our Mother the Church applies these words to the Blessed Virgin, "I am dark skinned and beautiful." It is possible that Simon of Cyrene, who helped Christ to carry the cross, was from Africa. Negro spirituals have enlightened all continents.

> Swing low, sweet chariot,
> Coming for to carry me home.
> If you get there before I do,
> Tell all my friends I'm coming too.
> I looked over Jordan, and what did I see?
> A band of angels coming after me,
> Coming for to carry me home.

Moonlit Marble

# Mother India

India is a great peninsula, bounded by the Bay of Bengal, the Arabian Sea and the Indian Ocean. It stretches about 1900 miles from the base of the triangle to the apex and is about the same length at its widest points. Some 400 million Indians represent 1/7 of the human race; they speak 845 dialects, of which 377 are in one State alone.

The religion of India is a hodgepodge. The largest group, the Hindus, believe more in birth and social conduct than in doctrine. Hinduism has no creed, no founder. It insists on the divinity of its own caste, the Brahmans. Thus it is defilement for a Brahman to contact the lower class, "the untouchables."

## Pakistan

Indian Mohammedans have long been at outs with Hindus. The partition of Pakistan set up a special country for the Muslims, although about 1/3 of the population of India proper still follows Mohammed. These disciples adhere to the teachings of the Koran, and to the principle, "There is one Lord, God Allah and Mohammed is his prophet."

The adherents to Buddhism deny the virtue of the caste system. They believe that sorrow and suffering are inevitable, that release is obtained by annihilation of any desires.

The Sikhs represent a powerful military organization. They began as a religious reform in 1500 A.D., which abolished the caste distinctions and refused to recognize the supremacy of the Brahmans. Their greatest shrine is the Golden Temple of Amritsar.

Another heterodox Hindu group is known as Jainism, which is in turn divided into several sects. They show excessive respect for the lives of animals and some assert that women cannot attain salvation.

The Parsees are adherents of the old Persian religion of Zoroaster, who fled to Bombay, India to escape Mohammedan persecution.

The influence of Animism is felt throughout the land. This is a belief that there are souls not only in men, but in stones, trees and animals. It is not known when or how the teaching of the transmigration of souls came to India. It has influenced all Hindu thought.

## Faith of Thomas

The Catholic Faith has been in parts of India since apostolic times. Saint Thomas, the Apostle, first brought the Faith to their country.

> The heavenly King's own warrior band,
> True lights to lighten every land.

The Church has received a petition from the Indian Christians to hasten the beatification of Sister Alphonsa. Christians in the Indian parliament, headed by Thomas Kottukapily of Meenachil, suggested: "No act in recent times could help so much the spread of the truth of Christianity in India as the raising of Sister Alphonsa to the altar."

In a Christian community of apostolic origin, in Bharananganam of the Diocese of Changanacherry, Travancore, Sister Alphonsa was born. The family name was characteristically sesquipedalian like many Indian words, a typesetter's delight, Muttathupadathu.

## Sister Alphonsa Muttathupadathu

When the Bishop of Changanacherry invested her with the holy habit of the Poor Claires on May 19, 1930, she remarked: "I joined the convent to become a saint, and having survived so many obstacles, what have I to live for if I don't become a saint?"

> Nature designed me for a life above
> The mere discordant dreams, in which I live.
> If I now go a beggar on the earth,
> I was Saint of heaven by right of birth.
> W. S. Blunt

Sister Alphonsa was relieved of a life-long cross in July, 1946. Mother India has millions of children, but few greater than Sister Alphonsa. Neither the Kashmir, the Himalayas, the Khyber Pass, the Ganges, nor the Taj Mahal surpass the beauty of her soul.

One of the greatest events in the history of India was the coming of Pope Paul VI to the Eucharistic Congress at Bombay. The Holy Father said, "We must meet not merely as tourists, but as pilgrims who set out to find God — not in buildings of stone but in human hearts; man must meet man, nation meet nation, as brothers and sisters, as children of God. In this mutual understanding and friendship, in this sacred communion we must also begin to work together to build the common future of the human race."

The most remarkable man of modern India was Mahatma Gandhi who said, during one of his political fasts: "God's voice has been increasingly audible as years have rolled by. He has never forsaken me even in my darkest hour. He has saved me often against myself and left me not a vestige of independence. The greater the surrender to Him the greater has been my joy."

# Behind the Bamboo

The approach of the Chinese New Year prompts reflections on the old years of China. This very paper must trace its origin back to the Chinese writing material, made of vertical strips of bamboo, or of silk. It was in the year 105 A.D. that a certain Ts'ai Lun reported to the emperor the possibility of using bark and rags.

From the Chinese the Arabs learned how to manufacture paper. They brought the knowledge to Egypt, where it replaced papyrus. Paper first entered Europe through Spain, thanks to the Moors, where it was made in 1150 A.D.

## Paper, Print, Porcelain

Paper soon led to the development of printing. By placing a moistened paper on an engraved stone and rubbing the raised portions with ink, an inscription could be duplicated. Thus the original "rubber stamp" was invented, when the Chinese used stamp-seals in the third century of the Christian era.

Like paper, Chinese printing passed into Europe, where a picture of St. Christopher was subscribed with two lines of block print.

The Chinese New Year also recalls the ancient use of lacquer in decorations. This sap of a Chinese tree was thick enough to be carved into designs.

The name China is a household word for porcelain. The genuine product is smooth, hard, translucent, and non-porous, China cups naturally suggest tea.

Teas
Where small talk dies in agonies. (Shelley)

The travels of tea can be found in the languages. The southern coastal areas of China call this drink, "te," and since it went west by water the word "the" is found in French and "tea" in English. North China calls the drink "ch'a" and tea which went by land is called "chai" in Russia, Persia, Turkey, and Greece.


## Tea, Herbs, Silk

The Chinese gave us not only much knowledge of medical herbs, but also flowers for our gardens. The camellia, China aster, chrysanthemum, peony, and azalea are from the good earth of the Orient.

The apricot, peach, and grapefruit have Chinese ancestors. The Dutch and the Germans call an orange the "Chinese apple."

Gutenberg's Bible was the first European printing with movable type. Although the Chinese also invented this more rapid method, they have retained block printing because of the nature of their written characters. Playing cards are Chinese.

> And my language is plain,
> That for ways that are dark
> And for tricks that are vain,
> The heathen Chinese is peculiar.
> — Bret Harte.


Only the Chinese knew how to make silk, and they kept the secret from about 1300 B.C. until 500 A.D. Silk was as valuable as gold in Rome and Constantinople; its light weight was pleasing to both merchant and camel. The well known Silk Road went by land through Turkestan and Persia to the Mediterranean Sea.

The Latins, with Virgil, thought that silk was combed from trees. It was some 500 years later that monks smuggled silkworm eggs out of China and announced to a startled Europe that the women's beautiful garments were the cocoons of caterpillars.

> How proud we are! how fond to shew
> Our clothes, and call them rich and new!
> When the poor sheep and silkworm wore
> That very clothing long before.
> — Isaac Watts

## Suzerains and Mandarins

The Chinese have always revered knowledge; the scholar was given the title of mandarin. In 1279 Pope Nicholas III sent five Franciscans to China. John of Monte Corvino built a cathedral at Peking, where he had seven auxiliary bishops in 1328, with a Catholic population of 30,000.

In 1579 Father Ricci, astronomer, mathematician, and linguist, entered China. His catechism became a classic in Chinese diction. His translation of Euclid earned for him the title of mandarin.

Likewise, Father Johann Adam Schall von Bell was named a mandarin of the first class, with the rank of prince. He became director of the Imperial Observatory and president of the Mathematical Institute.

Perhaps the Chinese character is represented in this story. A Chinese interpreter was translating on a blackboard the speech of a political dictator. When he was asked why he stopped writing the characters at many intervals, he replied: "We only write when the speaker says something."

Ping Pong and the visit of President Nixon to China indicated a day when the closed door will be open. Tourists who have looked upon Hong Kong, The Fragrant Harbor and Taiwan, Formosa the Beautiful, will see also the Grand Canal joining the Yellow River (China's Sorrow) and the Yangtse. They will walk on the streets of Shanghai, the Old Treaty Port, visit the Temple of Heaven in Peking and wonder at the Ming Tombs.

The Bamboo Curtain will be less lasting than the Great Wall of China. The household of the Faith will again be built on the good earth.

# Japanese St. Patrick's Day

It was on March 17, St. Patrick's Day, in 1865, that a French missionary, Pere Petitjean, was praying in a little chapel at Nagasaki. Three natives approached him and asked him three questions: "Have you a Pope? Do you pray to the Blessed Virgin? Are you married?" Having received satisfactory answers, they said, "Then you are a Christian like ourselves." They introduced the priest to 50,000 Japanese who had kept the Catholic faith for two centuries without a priest.

The land of this remarkable testimony to the faith is composed of four islands about equal in size to the state of California. Today it supports a population of 80,000,000 on a land that is 80 per cent mountainous, much of it of volcanic origin, with earthquakes and occasional tidal waves. The snow-covered Fuji adds its incomparable majesty to a beautiful countryside.

## Green Thumb

Ireland may be the emerald isle, but the Nipponese have the "green thumb." Every arable foot of earth is cultivated, and hillsides are terraced to produce rice in paddies. So precious is the soil that the farmer double-crops, for example, with wheat or barley. The Japanese have also perfected the art of bonsai, or dwarfing trees.

> Where soil is, men grow
> Whether to weeds or flowers.
> — Keats

These great horticulturists often wrap each fruit in tissue, so that the tree looks like cotton, with a growth of snow balls or popcorn. This care protects the fruit from both birds and insects.

For centuries the Nipponese planted mulberries, the food of silk worms. This was the land which led the world in the production of silk. Nylon eventually weakened the market, but it has since been found that silk may be blended with cotton and wool. It is doubtful if any synthetic will evoke such poetry as:

> Whenas in silks my Julia goes,
> Then, then (methinks) how sweetly flows
> That liquefaction of her clothes.
> — Robert Herrick

The Japanese are not only gardeners, but they are also the leading fishers of the world. Ranging far and wide they catch shellfish, cuttlefish, octopus, carp, sardines, tuna, swordfish, and herring. The nation consequently exports much seafood, both frozen and canned.

## Pearl Farmers

The people of Japan are also famous for pearl farming, a term which seems to blend their fishing ability with their agriculture. Diving girls bring up oysters from the sea, in which an irritant such as glass, or silver, is introduced. The oyster is then placed in an iron cage which is lowered into the ocean. Within seven years the mollusk has secreted a layer of nacre, a shelly concretion, as a defense against the foreign body.

The form of the pearl is variable. The color likewise may be black, blue, gray, purple, yellow, pink or white. The ideal gem is of a satiny luster, or silvery. Pearls may also be yielded by clams, conch shells, and mussels.

The ancients thought that pearls were formed by rain drops falling into open oysters and subsequently hardened by secretions.

> The liquid drops of tears that you have shed
> Shall come again, transformed to orient pearl
> (Richard III)

A Japanese menu may include tempura, seafood such as shrimp and prawns, deep fried in a batter. Raw fish, or sashimi, is a delectable food and seaweed also is palatable; sake is rice wine and sukiyaki is a tasty beef with vegetable cooked in an open skillet.

The general beverage of Japan is tea. It is the introduction to the home, the hotel, or the office. The drink is rather of the green tea than the black variety. The leaves of tea bushes are picked three or four times a year. The tea ceremony is a traditional social function, rigidly regulated by a ritual which requires precise training and graceful movements.

In this land of jujitsu shoes are left at the door, and a matted floor tatami is an excellent location for sleeping or eating.

> Tea does our fancy aid
> Repress those vapors which the head invade,
> And keeps the palace of the soul serene.
> — Ed Waller.

## Martyrs of Nagasaki

The first Europeans to arrive in Japan were the Portuguese in 1542. St. Francis Xavier and Jesuit missionaries came to the land of the rising sun in 1549. The rapid growth of Christianity was checked by a vicious persecution in 1597, when three Jesuits and six Franciscans were crucified at Nagasaki. In 1603 Japan closed its ports to all outsiders and became known as the "hermit nation." But, the Faith continued to grow until 1612 when all missionaries were driven from the country.

The door was forced open in 1853 by an American, Commodore Matthew C. Perry, who sailed into Tokyo Bay. Japan signed a treaty opening relationship with the world. Nagasaki has long been the ship-building yard, which sends ships around the world.

The Japanese are not mere imitators. The land of the Samurai sword has become one of the industrial giants of the world. The makers of dolls and woodblock printing have also produced much hydroelectric power and excellent transportation, the sumo-dogs and the sumo-wrestlers. The country of the Kamakura Buddha of bronze and the Daibutsu Budda, has rivaled Damascus in damascening with inlaid gold or silver.

In Japan is the well known carving at Nikko, which depicts three monkeys, one with hands over the eyes, a second covering his ears, and the third shielding his mouth. Originally they represented India, China, and Japan, but the world knows the simian threesome as "Hear no evil, speak no evil, see no evil."

As the scars of the atomic bombs have been gradually obliterated, so the martyrs of Nagasaki have been the seed of an expanding Faith. On St. Patrick's Day a Japanese catechizes, even as the faithful of Nagasaki quizzed the French Padre once on the 17th of March.

Doitashimashite! Sayonara!

*"Mabuhay"*

# Pearls of the Pacific

In the year 1520 four sailing boats might have been seen moving slowly through the stormy straits at the end of South America. The dominant voice of a man standing on the deck of the flagship might have been heard to say, "I name you All Saints Channel." For three weeks the little fleet crawled along the three hundred sevety-three miles of the channel, and then with a shout of joy, "thanking God and the Virgin Mary," the sailors saw before them a great body of water. Looking at the wrinkled sea, the captain said, "I christen thee Mar Pacifico, 'The Pacific Ocean.' " As other Spaniards later,

> He stared at the Pacific and all his men
> Looked at each other with a wild surmise
> (Keats)

For three months this intrepid mariner fixed his course towards the sunset sea, until at last he sighted land. On Easter Sunday, March 16, 1521, the natives of a certain island saw a priest offer the Holy Sacrifice of the Mass, and watched the fleet captain erect a cross on the nearby hill. The leader of that expedition was named Magellan; the island he called San Lazaro. Fifteen days later Magellan, the captain of the first ship to circumnavigate the globe, lost his life on one of the many islands.

## San Lazaro's Philippines

It was forty-four years after these events that four ships and a frigate put out from Mexico under Governor Miguel Lopez de Legaspi. In 1565 they landed on the shores which had received the footprints of Magellan and the 7100 islands of San Lazaro, green jewels in azure blue, were renamed the Philippines, after Philip II of Spain. In 1571 a convent was erected by the Augustinian Fathers and that was the beginning of the capital of Manila. Another St. Augustine's, on the island of Cebu, contains the Santo Nino, which dates back to the time of Magellan himself.

As soon as the missionaries became acquainted with the people they found very intelligent pupils. Quickly these capable characters absorbed the teaching of the Fathers. They learned to plant wheat, coffee, and potatoes. The use of cotton was introduced; the art of brickmaking and the employment of cement was quickly absorbed. A new alphabet and the science of printing were accepted by the Filipinos. This land of the ubiquitous bamboo exhibits rice terraces so elaborately elevated that they have been called the "eighth wonder of the world." This is a land of 70 languages and dialects, of sugar and coconut, boats called "Moro Vinta," turtle eggs, carabao and Manila hemp.

The ready intelligence of the island people is evident from the fact that the University of Santo Tomas was erected already in 1611. This is the oldest university which has existed under the American flag, for it was founded about twenty-three years before Harvard.

The stout-hearted Magellan brought the Cross to these natives; he assisted at Mass as soon as he had landed. Likewise, the second expedition brought the faith, which had been implanted at Vera Cruz and Mexico City. They carried the love of Mary, the Mother of God, for had not the Lady of the Californias, the Virgin who appeared at Guadalupe, been proclaimed Queen of all New Spain?

## Missa De Gallo

Nine days before Christmas in the Philippines, in the early dawn, people are walking to Church to attend the Missa de Gallo, the Mass of the Rooster. For them Christmas Eve is nine days long and during a novena of mornings they will attend the dawn Mass and exchange gifts. On the day of the Three Kings, children will put their shoes in the windows for the gifts of the Magi.

> Some say that ever 'gainst that season comes
> Wherein our Saviour's birth is celebrated,
> The bird of dawning singeth all night long . . .
> So hallowed and so gracious is the time.
> — Shakespeare

106

Or it may be Easter, and again the Filipino Christian shows his dramatic ability. A group of men is moving down the street carrying a statue of Christ. Up the street comes a procession of ladies bearing a statue of Mary, clothed in the black of death and sorrow. At the church door they stop, and from behind a curtain come the angelic voices of children, "Queen of Heaven, Rejoice, Alleluia, for He is Risen, as He said." The angel-children take from the Virgin the black veil, and clothe her with the white of joy.

## The Commonwealth

In 1898, the islands first came under the flag of the United States. Finally, on November 15, 1935, there came into existence the Philippine Commonwealth. With a background of such names as Admiral Dewey, William Howard Taft and General Douglas MacArthur, the republic was born on July 4, 1946. Thus the Philippines became independent from the United States, with which they had so many historical bonds.

It was a ship from Manila that really gave the name San Francisco to the beautiful bay of California. On July 5, 1595, Sebastian Cermenon sailed on the San Agustin across the same ocean named by Magellan. On November 6, he anchored at the Punta de los Reyes. He named the anchorage Bahia de San Francisco. After a search of one hundred thirty-seven years for this bay, the interior incomparable body of water behind the Golden Gate was discovered on All Souls Day.

> Once more I see Portola's cross uplifting
> Above the setting sun;
> And past the headland, northward, slowly drifting
> The freighted galleon.
> — Bret Harte

The land of the coconut, the ubiquitous bamboo, cockfighting, mat weaving, the barong Tagalog, the butterfly dress, the carabao, the rice terraces and the Malacanang Palace — welcomes, greets, and says farewell with the same word, "Mabuhay."

*Killing Time—*

# Teddy Bear

The sight of koalas in any zoo always assembles a large crowd at that attraction in the menagerie. Their babyish expression and our childhood memories of a Teddy Bear combine to make this Australian native a world favorite.

This native bear is, of course, not a bear at all; it belongs to the family of pouched mammals such as the kangaroo and the wombat. It was almost exterminated by men seeking the fur and within two years more than 250,000 koalas were ruthlessly slaughtered.

## The Australian Eucalyptus

The animal spends almost its entire life clinging to eucalyptus trees, its only food. This tree, which grows as tall as the California redwood, has been introduced into our state from "down under." The koala smells strongly like a eucalyptus cough drop because of the pungent oil absorbed in its exclusive diet.

Bipeds, who visit a zoo, often remark that the animals do nothing but sleep. Some animals doze during the day because they are nocturnal and, like the night shift, they must rest in daylight. All vertebrates, with the exception of birds, are accustomed to go into a comatose condition at certain periods.

Sleep that knits up the ravelled sleeve
of care,
The death of each day's life,
sore labor's bath.
— Shakespeare


Popular opinion thinks that winter-sleep is caused by cold. It imagines the body of an animal in a kind of frozen condition, like fish in ice. In this hypnotic state animals become very slow; the body grows rigid and sometimes can be rolled like a ball.


## Sleep

Hibernation, however, is occasioned not so much by low temperature as by lack of food. Thus some animals, living at 6000 feet, go into sleep during the month of August. The same species at a higher altitude, where there is more cold and more food, do not retire until September.

Cold is, at most, a secondary factor in hibernation. Even the accumulation of excessive fat does not explain the advent of sleep. Only one thing is clear, that winter-sleep is a means of preserving life, when starvation threatens.

The phenomenon of winter, called hibernation, also occurs in summer and is known as aestivation. Summer-sleep is caused among fishes and reptiles more by lack of water than by need of food.

The most famous aestivator is the lung-fish. When the drought threatens, this fish dives into the mud and covers its head with the tail. The skin soon exudes a layer of mucus which enveloped the body. The fish thus closes its gill opening and uses its mouth to breathe through a tube of clay.

The wisdom of the Creator brings creatures to hibernation and aestivation for preserving life, when food and water are scarce. The habit has become so natural to some species that in captivity they fall asleep on schedule, even when the zoo-keeper has food for them.

An animal fulfills its destiny when it procreates the species and plays its part in the balance of nature. Man, however, acts humanly when he generates an idea and when he falls in love with good. When the intellect attains a truth and the will loves a good, then is man the rational animal.

Man sleeps for about one third of his life. A koala bear, stuffed with eucalyptus leaves, may sleep comfortably on the fork of a precarious branch. By sleep a nocturnal animal can prowl and forage at night. By sleep man strengthens his body that it may be a fit instrument of his soul.

## Down Under

The koala is also known in Australia as the "native sloth." This Teddy Bear, however, wastes little time in carrying out the design of the Creator. Sloth is one of the capital sins of homo sapiens; it is also called "killing time."

The animal sleeps and only consumes body fat. When man sleeps through the night and sweats through the day, he can earn heaven by saying morning and night prayers. Prayers may take any form, original or borrowed.

> Seven hours to thought,
> To soothing slumber seven;
> Ten to the world allot,
> And all to heaven.

Australia, the down-under continent, is about the size of the United States. Its national animal is not only the koala, but also the kangaroo, the emu, the duck-billed platypus and the wallaby. Characteristic birds are the cassowary, the lyre bird and the notorious kookaburra, a kingfisher commonly known as the laughing jackass. The country abounds in eucalyptus and wattles, sheep and sea life, sheep dogs and dingoes. Baobabs are trees with strange trunks known as "bottle trees"; the "outback" has little vegetation.

The long sought lost continent was known as terra australis incognita, but Australia is a growing country of cities like Sydney, Melbourne, and Brisbane with many millions of "downunders."

> Hear a raucous sound of laughter
>    from the nearby quiet wood
> Where the kookaburras praise the Lord
>    who made the world so good.

*Ship Of Pearl*

# Skeleton Islands

Here in the Pacific we seem to be surrounded by islands. An island is a piece of land surrounded by water. There are two kinds of islands, continental and oceanic. The former are intimately joined with the mainland. Sometimes a coast settles and submerges, so that the summits of its mountains remain above water. Perhaps the neck of an isthmus, or peninsula, is worn out by erosion and the sea cuts through the land.

Thus, if the ocean broke through to the bay, south of the City, San Francisco would be an island. It seems that the ocean opened the Golden Gate and flooded the valley of the bay. Alcatraz, Angel and Goat Islands are simply the crests of hills.

Oceanic islands are those whose base belongs in structure to the ocean bed. Some bodies are of volcanic origin; these push up rather suddenly even as a land volcano. The Hawaiian Islands are of volcanic nature and some of the craters are periodically active.

Much of the Malay Archipelago is both continental and oceanic, but the Carolines are truly oceanic. The Marianas are both volcanic and coralline limestone.

Perhaps the most interesting island is the coralline. Swimmers in tropical waters are familiar with the very sharp material, hidden below the surface, on which they sometimes cut their feet. The same substance ornaments many mantles.

Pliny tells us that Gauls used to decorate their war helmets with coral. The ancient Romans gathered coral from the Mediterranean Sea and hung it about their necks as an amulet against danger.

## Angel Skin

The color of coral differs much in each locality. Some is white as chalk and in the Persian gulf is coral, black as coal. There was once a Mediterranean trade with India, where some thought this substance of the sea had medical properties.

The red or precious coral of the sea is most beautiful. The Italians speak of pale flesh coral, "pelle d'angelo," skin of angels. This "skin of angels," however, is only the skeleton of animals. The Greeks called the pink coral, *gorgeia,* associating it with the head of Medusa, which was supposed to turn to stone all who looked at her.

The song of Ariel in Shakespeare's Tempest is poetic license with science:

> Full fathom five thy father lies;
> Of his bones are coral made;
> These are pearls that were his eyes;
> Nothing of him that doth fade
> But doth suffer a sea-change
> Into something rich and strange.

Coral is simply a collection of countless skeletons of the polyp. A polyp is not a fish, a shrimp, or an insect, but a small marine organism. It secretes a skeleton composed of carbonate of lime, limestone. These bodies begin to stack up row on row, like niches of a columbarium. Dead coral, at the bottom, turns brown or black and is called burnt coral. Some polyp branches like shrubs. Others spread like a fan and especially under water look like flowers.

## Not Atoll

There are three kinds of coral reefs — barrier, fringing, and atoll. Before the war in the Pacific very few Americans would have discovered the word "atoll" in their crossword puzzles.

When General MacArthur began hopping, skipping and jumping to Tokyo, when the Navy spoke of ships hidden in atolls, and when assaulting Marines were hung up on a reef — everybody knew of the atolls.

A coral reef inclosing a lagoon is known as an atoll. Here fleets may lie, even as

> . . . the ship of pearl which, poets feign,
> Sails the unshadowed main —
> The venturous bark that flings
> On the sweet summer wind its purpled wings
> In gulfs enchanted, where the siren sings,

And coral reefs lie bare,
Where the cold sea-maids rise to sun their streaming hair.
— Oliver W. Holmes

The fauna and flora of islands is naturally very different. On one side of a Pacific line, plants and animals are distinctly Asiatic. On the other side life is descended from Australia.

It is not without reason that the small isolated islands may have palm trees. The tree throws off a cocoanut. This is really a seed, outfitted in a fibrous jacket, which is buoyant as a life-preserver. The ship of life may float thousands of miles to another island. Soon we have the desert island with the palm trees, of which we dream each year as vacation time approaches.

## Isles of the Blest

The Isles of the Blest are a place where, according to story, the virtuous are transported without death.

Come, my friends,
'Tis not too late to seek a newer world.
Push off, and sitting well in order smite
The sounding furrows; for my purpose holds
To sail beyond the sunset, and the baths
Of all the western stars, until I die.
It may be that the gulfs will wash us down:
It may be we shall touch the Happy Isles.
— Alfred Lord Tennyson

But even romantic islands are very prosaic. The GI saw no poetry in mosquitos, rain, mud, heat, insects, sunburned sirens. Poets of the Pacific never described our heavenly home as well as a man named Paul: "Eye has not seen nor ear heard, nor has it entered into the heart of man, to imagine what thing God has prepared for those who love Him."

I know not where His islands lift
Their fronded palms in air;
I only know I cannot drift
Beyond His love and care.
— John Whittier.

Of the many Pacific islands those which are inhabitable have been divided for convenience into three classes. One group is known as Micronesia, with such islands as the Gilberts, Ellices, and Marianas. Another is called Polynesia, represented by Hawaii, Samoa, the Tonga, the Marquesas, the Cook Islands and the Societies. Those settled by the negroid race are embraced in the name Melanesia, which includes the Solomons, New Guinea, New Hebrides, Fiji and Caledonia.

The lingua franca of Oceania is pidgin english, which is easily learned and understood over the vast Pacific. Thus the Lord's Prayer in pidgin becomes:

Papa belong me, he live him long topside heaven.
Name belong you, he good.

*Birds of a feather*

# South American Washington

Jose de San Martin, born in South America about the time that George Washington was winning independence in North America, was the liberator of three nations.

The eagle has been adopted as the symbol of the United States. For the sake of biography, let the South American condor be expressive of San Martin.

The large size of the condor reminds us of the extensive accomplishments of Jose. The bird is perhaps the largest of all the winged creatures of the air. It may be about four feet long and measure 10 feet between the wing tips.

Like a condor, San Martin moved across three countries to which the power of his person brought the freedom of earth and sky.

## Andes and Argentine

The eagle of the Andes begins its life high in the mountains, where a nest of a few sticks holds two white eggs, about four inches long. In seven weeks the shell breaks to reveal a young bird, covered with a whitish down. It will be a year later before the fledgling will attempt its first flight from the lofty perch.

The young will then be almost as large as the parents, with a plumage of black, except for a frill of white feathers at the base of the neck, and a few white patches on the wings.

San Martin was born in the land of the condors, at Yapeyu in Argentina. Five children lived in the rugged home amid the big forests, where the father, a Spanish officer, reared his family.

> As a bird each fond endearment tries
> To tempt its new-fledged offsprings to the skies,
> He tried each art, reproved each dull delay
> Allured to brighter worlds, and led the way.
> — Oliver Goldsmith.

When his father was transferred to Spain, Jose followed and in time became a cadet in the army. He wore the uniform of Spain until he was 30 years old.

But like a bird of the mountains, the feelings of San Martin were in America, where a spirit of independence was tempting the newborn to the skies of freedom.

## Chile and Peru

The subsequent movements of San Martin were swift like the condor. He became president in the triumvirate of La Plata; he formed the Lautaro lodge and united the factions of Buenos Aires. His spirit prevailed at the Congress of San Miguel de Tucuman.

Jose led mounted grenadiers into the mountain passes of the Andes, the home of the condors. He knew that the freedom of the Argentine required the independence of her neighbors.

At the battles of Chacabuco and Maipu, he achieved the freedom of Chile.

The extraordinary force of his person is indicated when he, an Argentinian, continued to lead an army of Chileans into Peru. The capital, Lima, acclaimed San Martin as its liberator.

> The distant mountains, that uprear
> Their solid bastions to the skies,
> Are crossed by pathways, that appear
> As we to higher levels rise.

The size and flying range of the condor recall the greatness and extensive influence of San Martin. A second characteristic of the bird is its endurance.

It has been said that the condor can live 40 days without food. While it can glide for an hour with no perceptible flutter of its massive wings, it must struggle and frequently flap to reach the higher air.

Before San Martin attained prominence, he had to show much endurance. He suffered from ill health all during his life. The forced

120

marches over mountains, scarcity of food, and battle fatigue would have killed a less virile soul.

> The heights by great men reached and kept,
> Were not attained by sudden flight,
> But they, while their companions slept,
> Were toiling upward in the night.
> — Josiah Holland

Like the bird of the Andes, San Martin withdrew from the human scene. He left the glory of Chile to his fellow soldier, Bernardo O'Higgins.

## Sublime Abdication

After meeting Simon Bolivar at Gauyaquil, San Martin made a sublime decision. From the height of his great personality, he viewed the whole panorama. He decided that he would best serve three nations by retiring from the scene.

San Martin sailed for Europe, leaving South America to Simon Bolivar.

The natural blessings of South America are as extensive as the great continent itself. There are grassy llanos, orchids and tree-matted selvas. Angel Falls is the highest in the world; the ancient civilization of the Incas is found in the mountains. There are balsa and bananas, coffee and salt mines. There is bauxite and timber, savannas and pampas, even fjords.

Such is the enchanting land of the gaucho, the tango, the giant tortoises and lizards, volcanoes, parrots and penguins.

In his 73rd year the soul of San Martin flew to its Creator. Quitting his body on the soil of France, he expressed a wish that his heart might rest in Buenos Aires.

No man is either an eagle or condor. Man is capable of soaring only with the soul, his mind and will. The heights of liberty were attained by the noble struggle of great men.

*Como Un Astro*

# Empress of Mexico

Every nation of the world seems to have its shrine to the Blessed Virgin, but no nation has been so completely identified with Mary as Mexico. The only self-portrait of the Mother of God ever given to man was presented to Mexico. In the words of the Holy Father, "she has not done so to any other nation."

A plaque donated by Pope Leo XIII states in Latin verse:

> Here, beloved Mother, beneath your miraculous image,
>> The Mexican people are happy to pay you homage
>> And to profit by your loving protection.
> By your aid, may they always happily flourish,
>> And with you as Patroness, may they ever preserve
>> Firm and unshaken the faith of Christ.

This was the land of the Aztecs, recalled in the flag which shows an eagle perched on a cactus, with a snake in its beak. Their civilization is remembered in the pyramid of the sun, larger than Cheops of Egypt. This is the land of volcanoes, from the extinct Ixtaccihuatl to the active Popocatepetl, from Popo and Izzy to the very new Paricutin which pushed up only in 1943.

For these reasons it is necessary to descend in order to reach Mexico City, whether the traveler comes by air or by auto. Built on the bowl of a huge lake bed, the area is gradually sinking beneath the mash of volcanic ash and water. Mexico abounds in bananas, vanilla, beans, tobacco, cocoa, copper, lead, zinc, gold, coal, opals and silver.

## Juan of Guadalupe

To this land came Hernan Cortes on Good Friday, April 21, 1519, when he landed at Vera Cruz. It was only forty years after the discovery of Columbus that Mary, the Mother of God, visited a hill near Mexico City, known as Tepeyac. The place is known as Guadalupe which, it is said, means "she who crushes the serpent." Mary made her visit in this wise:

On December 9, 1531, an Indian named Juan Diego, 57 years old, was confronted by a lady as he walked towards town. Her message to the Aztec was, "Here I will listen to tears and prayers and will give consolation. Go to the Bishop of Mexico City and tell him to build a church here."

Bishop Juan de Zumarraga heard the story with sympathy, but with a prudent doubt. He asked that Juan Diego obtain some tangible evidence of his meeting with a lady who made such an important request. On the occasion of his fourth encounter with the lady, Juan was told, in mid-winter, to cut some Castilian roses and take them to the bishop.

## Painted in Heaven

Arriving at the bishop's house, the Indian opened his cloak, or tilma, to deliver the roses. He was surprised when His Excellency fell on his knees before him and gazed intently at the garment. What the bishop saw in 1531 may be viewed today above the high altar at Guadalupe.

The tilma is a garment about six feet by three feet made up of two strips, each eighteen inches wide. These are stitched together. The material itself is a loosely woven sack-like covering of very coarse quality, a serape of sisal, maguey cactus. On the tilma is a picture, painted in some mysterious way, with no brush marks visible even under a microscope. It seems to be partly oil, partly of water colors distemper and stain of flowers.

The artist certainly selected a poor "canvas," without sizing, a material which naturally might last from 20 to 30 years. For a century the picture was exposed to the elements, without its present glass protection. Neither the fog from the nearby salt lake nor the smoke of countless votive candles have obliterated the figure. No human painter of the time could have learned such excellency from the Aztec-Maya-Toltec art, nor from the Spanish culture of that date. The creator of this masterpiece disappeared completely and no other work of this hand has ever been found. A good human artist would surely have other contemporary works, which would easily show a relationship.

## The Second Eve

The face of the lady is oval, dark-skinned. It could easily be the actual features of Mary of Nazareth. The gown is rose-colored, traced with patterns of roses and lilies. The sleeves and neck are faced with white rabbit fur. From the body 120 golden rays project. Her hands are folded in prayer; she wears a gold brooch with a black cross in the center. The mantle is blue-green, with rays of 48 stars, each of 8 points.

It is probable that if a title is to be given to the picture, it would be Mary of the Immaculate Conception. Beneath her is the crescent moon, with the angel, Michael. She is the woman of the Apocalypse "clothed with the sun, standing on the moon with a crown of stars on her mantle."

> Spell Eva back and Ave you shall find
> The first began, the last reversed our harms;
> An Angel's witching words did Eva bind,
> An Angel's Ave disenchants the charms.
> Death first by Woman's weakness entered in.
> In Woman's virtue Life doth now begin.
> — Robert Southwell

Since that day when Mary visited Mexico, thousands upon thousands of pilgrims, Indians, mestizos, whites and visitors from foreign lands, have offered their homage at this famous shrine. All eyes focus on the tilma of Juan Diego, with its heavenly picture clearly visible to the kneeling suppliant. It is said that the reflected image of Juanito can be seen in the pupils of the Virgin.

Tourists may be interested in the Zocalo, the square before one of the largest cathedrals in America, or in the floating gardens of Xochimilco, Grasshopper Hill, and the famous Halls of Montezuma commemorated in the Marine Hymn.

The volcanic peaks tell the geological story of the land; the pyramids stand as witness to the Mayan and Aztec civilization. Mexico is the country of the tortilla, the pole dancer, chiclet chewing gum, the California adobe and Mission tile, the maguey or century plant. The cynosure of all, however, is not Acapulco, Taxco, Guadalajara or Chihuahua, but the Virgin of Guadalupe is the miraculous magnet.

> De la Santa Montana en la cumbre
> Parecio como un astro Maria,
> Uhuyentando con placida lumbre
> Las tinieblas de la idolatria.
>
> Mexicanos volad presurosos
> Del penden de la Virgen en pos,
> Den la lucha, saldreis victoriosos
> Defendiendo a la Patria y a Dios.

*Maple Leaf Forever*

# The St. Lawrence

The St. Lawrence waterway project includes the largest body of fresh water in the world. If you were a leaf and could ride the course from source to mouth, you would start the voyage on a plateau in Minnesota. This region is likewise the origin of the Mississippi, which flows to the Gulf of Mexico, and the Red River, which runs north to the Hudson Bay.

The leaf floats into Lake Superior, which is 602 feet above sea level, the largest link in the chain. The water falls about 22 feet through St. Mary's River into Lake Huron.

## Sault Sainte Marie

This is the site of the oldest settlement in Michigan, Sault Sainte Marie, named after the Blessed Virgin by Jogues and Rambault.

St. Mary's river is 63 miles long; the rapids are about a half mile wide and ¼ mile long. It takes a ship from 12 to 20 minutes to navigate the locks. Traffic through this waterway exceeds that of the Panama, Suez, Kiel, and Manchester canals combined.

> The river knows the way to the sea,
> Without a pilot it runs and falls,
> Blessing all lands with its charity.

Lake Huron receives not only the water from Superior, through the Sault Sainte Marie, but also of Lake Michigan through the Strait of Mackinac. The floating leaf of Minnesota continues its Odyssey through the St. Clair river and Lake to the Detroit river, where it enters Lake Erie.

A leaf has no difficulty dropping 326 feet from Lake Erie over Niagara Falls into Lake Ontario. This water is now 234 feet above the sea when it bursts into the bed of the St. Lawrence river. Down to Montreal the channel is about 300 feet wide and 28 feet deep.

Fed by great tributaries such as the Ottawa river, which is 800 miles long, the St. Lawrence at times is four miles wide. And so the leaf, which voyaged from the forests above Lake Superior, floats past the rock of Quebec, where the St. Lawrence is a kind of estuary finally expanding to about 60 miles.

## The Rock of Quebec

The voyage ends in the Gulf of St. Lawrence, where the buoyant leaf completes a distance of more than 2000 miles and enters the Atlantic Ocean.

> I hurry amain to reach the plain
> Run the rapid and leap the fall
> Split at the rock and together again
> Accept my bed, narrow or wide.
> — Sydney Lanier

Like the leaf, man has long been able to make this same voyage. At first there were many portages with canoes; later locks and canals, opened the passage to steam ships. However, present conditions limit the vessels to a 14-foot draught and 270-foot length.

In 1534 Jacques Cartier sailed into this Gulf of St. Lawrence. He navigated the river as far as the site of Quebec and Montreal. Just beyond Montreal are the rapids named Lachine, a word for China. The dream of many early explorers was to find a waterway to the East Indies.

On August 10, Cartier called the water after the saint of the day, Lawrence. He was one of the most famous of a long list of martyrs. As early as 257 A.D. dictators knew that the best attack on the Church was to kill the Bishops. When Pope St. Sixtus was led to execution, he was followed by Lawrence.

Lawrence said to him: "Father, where are you going without your son? Should the priest go to sacrifice without the deacon?" The Pope answered: "I do not leave you. You will follow me in three days."

128

## Lawrence the Deacon

Some thieves think that the vessels of the Church are of priceless value. The emperor said to Lawrence: "I am informed that your priests offer in gold, that the Sacred Blood is received in silver cups and that you have wax tapers fixed in golden candlesticks. Bring out these hidden treasures."

In a few days Lawrence assembled all the poor of the city, who were supported by the Church. He then said to the dictator: "These are the treasures of the Church."

In anger Valerian ordered Lawrence to be stripped and bound to a gridiron. After extreme suffering the martyr smiled and said: ' Let my body be turned; one side is broiled enough."

Since the name St. Lawrence was the first given to this river, countless shrines have been erected along its course. The Cathedral of Quebec once embraced a diocese from Canada to Mexico. Canada now stretches from the Plains of Abraham to Lake Louise, from the Rock of Quebec to the Pacific, from the Great Lakes to the Arctic Circle.

St. Lawrence looks from his heaven upon his river where faithful gather at shrines of St. Anne-de-Beaupre, Cap-de-la-Madeleine, St. Joseph's Oratory, and the Church of Notre Dame.

When Thomas Moore heard the river boatmen singing in French, which he could not understand, he translated the melody into his own ideas.

Faintly as tolls the evening chime,
Our voices keep tune and our oars keep time.
Soon as the woods on shore look dim,
We'll sing at St. Ann's our parting hymn.
Row, brothers, row, the stream runs fast,
The Rapids are near, and the daylight past.

# A Small Country

Seldom can an entire country be viewed in one glance from an airplane. However, the width and breadth of Vatican City can be embraced in one look from the air. Perhaps the human eye has never seen so much in so little, so much history and art within 108 acres.

There is the great square of St. Peter, a piazza in the form of an ellipse, with a breadth of 645 feet. It is set off by the famous Colonnade of Bernini, consisting of 248 columns in 4 rows, surmounted by 162 statues. From the plane the edifice does not seem so large, but the Colonnade is 57 feet wide and 75 feet high; while the statues themselves are 12 feet. Between the rows of columns there is space wide enough for carriages. Clearly visible in the center of the square is an obelisk, which formerly stood in Nero's Circus and now marks the spot where Peter, the first Pope, was crucified in the year 67 A.D.

## The Martyr's Tomb

No aviator in the world could miss the landmark which looks on the square of St. Peter.

> But lo! the dome, the vast and wonderous dome,
> To which Diana's marvel was a cell!
> Christ's mighty shrine, above His martyr's tomb!
> But thou, of temples old, or altar new,

Standest alone — with nothing like to thee —
Worthiest of God, the holy and the true.
                                    — Lord Byron

The facade of the mighty temple is 357 feet wide and 114 feet high. Eight travertine columns, 93 feet high and 8 feet in diameter may be seen, surmounted by a balustrade on which are statues of Christ and the Apostles, each 19 feet in height. But lo! the dome of St. Peter's lifts its lantern 421 feet into the heavens. It is surmounted by a ball, which is in turn topped by a cross, 453 feet, and within that very ball there is room for sixteen persons.

The flying passengers see only the outer shell of Peter's tomb. The pedestrians far below in the square might enter the great cathedral.

Enter: its grandeur overwhelms thee not;
And why? it is not lessen'd; but thy mind,
Expanded by the genius of the spot
Has grown colossal.
Thou seest not all; but piecemeal thou must break
To separate contemplation, the great whole.

The eye looks forward down the nave of the church, a distance of 619 feet; it measures the transept 449 feet, it falls upon the canopy of Bernini. This canopy itself lifts its 700 tons to the height of 95 feet; below it lies the body of the first Pope. The visitor's eye quickly climbs from the tomb to the cupola, a distance of 438 feet, with an inside diameter of 139 feet.

## Upon This Rock

Around the great circle one may read in Latin, "Thou art Peter and upon this rock I will build My Church, and I will give to thee the keys to the Kingdom of Heaven." The letters themselves are in mosaic on a gold background and are five feet in height. These words spoken to Peter look down upon the famous statue of St. Peter, whose bronze foot is literally worn out by the multiplied kisses of millions of pilgrims.

Hidden from view of the air is the famous Pieta of Michelangelo, which rests in one of the many chapels. This is the only work of the great genius which bears his name, for one day, angered by people who were speculating concerning the possible author of the Pieta, the master grabbed his scalpel and scratched on the band, which crossed the Virgin's breast, "Michelangelo." When told that his Virgin Mary was too young, he replied, "Chastity enjoys eternal youth."

This great Church was 176 years in building; it can contain 60,000 people; it offers for study 34 altars, 396 statues of marble, bronze and

132

stucco; 748 columns of stone, marble, alabaster and bronze. Furthermore, besides the body of St. Peter, this church contains the major relics of Christendom.

> Majesty, Power, Glory, Strength,
> and Beauty, all are aisled
> In this eternal ark of worship undefiled.

## The Muses

Close to St. Peter's is the Museum of Paintings, which consists of fifteen halls. The flying pilots can not see the famous works of Raphael, the Transfiguration, the Madonna of Foligno, the Crowning of the Virgin and his famous tapestry, the Miraculous Fishing. This museum also contains the Communion of St. Jerome by Domenichino and the Crucifixion of St. Peter by Reni.

The Transfiguration, considered by many the greatest painting in the world, was exposed unfinished at the head of the death-bed of Raphael on Good Friday. He died looking at the Transfiguration and it was finished by his pupils.

Also close to St. Peter's is the Sistine Chapel, built between the years 1473 and 1484; it is here that the election of a new pope takes place. On the great wall behind the altar is the celebrated scene of the Last Judgment, by Michelangelo, which is 66 feet high and 33 feet wide. The ceiling of the chapel is covered with biblical frescoes by the same genius.

The Vatican Library was begun by Pope Nicholas V in 1450; it contains 500,000 volumes and 53,000 manuscripts. No books are visible since they are all enclosed in illuminated cupboards. Among its priceless originals and manuscripts are a Greek Bible of the 4th century and the Codex Vaticanus; the Homilies of Gregory the Great; the manuscripts of Virgil, Cicero and Terence; the Memologium, a sacred calendar of the 10th century; the Divina Commedia of Dante; the Affirmation of the Seven Sacraments by Henry VIII, for which ironically, the King of England still calls himself Defender of the Faith.

> O Rome illustrious, of the world empress!
> Over all the cities thou queen in thy goodliness!
> Red with the roseate blood of the martyrs, and
> White with the lilies of virgins at God's right hand!
> Welcome we wing to thee; ever we bring to thee
> Blessings, and pay to thee praise for eternity.
> (Pilgrim Song 9th century)

*This little "O"*

# This Little Globe

So quickly do the astronauts circle the globe that it seems indeed a small world. That the earth is a sphere was suggested as early as 640 B.C. by Thales. He even divided the sphere into five climatic zones, with a terminology which we still use. It was also known, at that early time, that the earth rotates on its own axis.

Popular opinion, however, showed little accurate knowledge of the earth. Scandinavian myths referred to the universe as a tree, which supported the earth in its branches.

Hindus considered the world as a platter, supported by four elephants, which stood on the back of a turtle. For the Greeks the sun was a fiery chariot racing across the sky.

> The unwearied sun, from day to day
> Does his Creator's power display,
> And publishes to every land
> The work of an almighty hand.
>      — Joseph Addison

The first known model of a revolving sphere was made by Crates in the second century before Christ. Many had long suspected that the earth was a ball. They had noticed that the horizon is circular, that ships disappeared gradually by hulls, sails, and topmasts. In time, some pointed to the curved shadow of the earth during the eclipse of the moon.

## Spinning Spheres

The most practical demonstration of the earthly sphere was to travel around it. The first ships to circumnavigate the globe were in the expedition of Magellan in 1522.

Mother Earth has been accurately measured by man; he finds that the diameter of the equator is 7926.68 miles, about three times the width of the United States.

The circumference of the globe is 24,902 miles, which a non-stop airplane would circle in 8 days and 16 hours, at the speed of only 120 miles an hour.

## The Creator's Marbles

The earth-ball is a very heavy globe, spun from the finger tips of the Creator at a speed of 18½ miles per second, on a 600-million-mile orbit. And this is one of the smaller spheres which Omnipotence set in motion!

To number its weight in tons, simply write the number 66, followed by 21 zeros. It reads six sextillion, six hundred and sixty quintillion tons.

> This is a piece too fair
> To be the child of chance, and not of care.
> No atoms casually together hurled
> Could e'er produce so beautiful a world.
> — John Dryden

Man finds his way around the earth by marking the ball with lines. The latitudes run parallel to the equator, and we count them in degrees north or south, until they reach 90 at the North and South Poles.

We navigate east and west from a vertical line which passes through Greenwich, England, where the British Royal Observatory was established in 1675. This prime meridian is 0, and the longitudes ascend until we reach 180 degrees west or east, halfway around the globe.

Since the earth is a ball, the shortest route around it is along the great circle, which divides the globe into two parts. If you measure distance with a string, you may stretch the string on the equator, noting the degrees. There each degree is 69.16 miles in length, and this figure, multiplied by degrees, gives the mileage.

## More Magellans

In 1924 U.S. military planes rounded the world in 15 days, 11 hours, and 7 minutes. The Graf Zeppelin circled the earth in 20 days and

136

4 hours. The northern circle was traversed by Post and Gatty in 8 days, 15 hours, and 51 minutes.

In 1949, the first nonstop, round-the-world flight was made by Lucky Lady, a B-59, in 94 hours and 1 minute. On a flat map voyages and flights may seem to be roundabout, but the circle course is always the quickest way to move around. Thus, at one time in 45 hours B-52's saw California, Newfoundland, French Morocco, North Africa, India, Ceylon, the Philippines, Guam, and California. Now the jet planes and the space capsules have contracted time and space.

This earthly sphere became important when the Creator became a baby in Bethlehem. On one of its rocks, shaped like a skull, the Redeemer was crucified.

At His death even the earth quaked and the rocks were rent.

Man can circle the globe only after God has created both him and earth.

> Nature and nature's laws
> Lay hid in night;
> God said, "Let Newton be,"
> And all was light.
> — Alexander Pope

# Homesick

### Germany

Unter den Linden is a name
World famous, but all the same
When a friend I wish to meet
Give me a San Francisco street.

### France

Les rues of France are broad and gay
And grander still Champs Elysees
But be it cold or be there heat
Show me a San Francisco street.

### Austria

Vienna's Ring is justly famous
For me it's simply not the same as
Market, Mission, a policeman's beat
On any San Francisco street.

### Spain

Madrid's Gran Via has its points
But no trottoir or bistro joints
Can please me when I plan to eat
As dining on San Francisco's street.

### England

The Strand or Picadilly Circus
Have crowds and traffic there to irk us,
With rested or tourist tired feet
Let me walk a San Francisco street.

### Italy

Piazza and sculpture and cultured Rome
Forums, paintings and catacombs
Nor council, nor Pope, makes the heart beat
Like a home at nearby Dolores Street.

Publisher

willow house

Stockton, California

Photography by
Kenichi James Nakata
Stockton, California

Layout and Design by
dot Design, San Francisco

Printing and Binding by
Bradford Printing
Denver, Colorado 80202